CHRIST'S WAIT FOR GODOT

A THEOLOGICAL APPRECIATION OF SAMUEL BECKETT

STEPHEN D. MORRISON

BELOVED PUBLISHING • COLUMBUS, OHIO

Beloved Publishing • Columbus, Ohio

Print ISBN: 978-1-63174-179-1

eBook ISBN: 978-1-63174-180-7

Acknowledgements:

I am deeply indebted to Jürgen Moltmann. When I wrote to you in 2017 about this book, I had no idea it would take so long. But your encouraging letter was a constant source of strength on the days I felt it might never come into being. Thank you for your patience. As I hope this book shows, your work has continued to inspire me endlessly. And I am forever grateful for the impact your theology has had on my life and thinking.

CONTENTS

Introduction v

1. He Leaves No Maggot Lonely 1
2. She Rails at the Source of All Life 29
3. Unspeakable Home 51
4. I Can't Go On, I'll Go On 81

Conclusion 103
Notes 109
Bibliography 119
Also by Stephen D. Morrison 127

INTRODUCTION

The only certainty in life is uncertainty; the only constant is chaos. Shallow versions of faith and theology try to mitigate mystery by offering cheap answers to hard questions. We deceive ourselves into believing security might come from a book, dogma, system, or tradition. But genuine faith resists all bargain answers. To fully seek the truth is to stare uncertainty straight in the eye, to wrestle with it. It is *because* life is uncertain that faith is necessary. Faith looks like Job on his heap of tears and ashes debating God and man, Abraham strapping Isaac to a sacrificial altar, and Jacob limping for the rest of his life after wrestling with God. What Christians today have forgotten is that faith is dangerous. *Faith is a risk.*

Samuel Beckett has wrestled with God, truth, and meaning perhaps more fervently than any other modern writer. His courage to challenge shallow certainties is one of the many reasons why his work remains so compelling. Beckett's writing illustrates what true faith looks like in practice, its struggles and lamentations, but also its raw beauty. Thus, his work comforts those struggling along the path of faith and the quest for meaning—regardless of what, if any, creed they confess.

Beckett was neither a theologian nor a religious man in the traditional sense of the word, but he was, as John Pilling aptly stated, a "God-haunted" man. It is often wrongly assumed that Beckett was faithless—as if the opposite of belief is unbelief and the inverse of faith is doubt. But these are false alternatives, and Beckett defies all such labels.

John Calder helpfully explains the paradox of Beckett's faith:

> [H]e cannot be described as a believer, a non-believer, an atheist or even an agnostic. He disbelieved with a large doubt or disbelieved reluctantly or, more accurately, he kept the belief and disbelief poised in his mind, always unresolved, while he went on consciously speculating about the nature and the existence of God.[1]

Beckett's writing expresses the struggle of faith in the pursuit of an unnamable truth. Contrary to common interpretations of Beckett, I aim to show how his spiritual sensibilities go beyond a shallow engagement with religious symbols as mere symbols, and instead, is itself a kind of faith seeking understanding, however paradoxical. His work is deeply spiritual in a strange but profound way. I think Calder was correct to conclude, "Beckett lost his faith logically, but not emotionally."[2] There is a spiritual depth to Beckett's quest for God in God-forsaken spaces, for human solidarity in the pit of human suffering, and hope in hopelessness.

The pursuit of truth is costly; it is an unpaved path. Faith and doubt are not enemies but allies in that pursuit. Faith, without doubt, professes allegiance to dogma rather than awe before a vast mystery. It is a shallow faith. That is how I would define fundamentalism: the desire for truth without mystery—a namable, controllable truth.[3] Yet the inverse is also true: doubt without some sense of the unknown—such as scientism and its delusion of disproving God—is just another form of fundamentalism, of demystifying the universe with cheap answers. But the world is not black and white; it is grey, so it is inexplicable.

Beckett's words have significantly shaped my life. But it is sometimes difficult to justify my admiration. I am a Christian who has somehow found a wellspring of spiritual comfort and hope in the bleak and blasphemous words of Samuel Beckett. As strange as it may sound, I am inescapably drawn to his work, not *in spite of* how dark it is at times, but *because* of its relentless wallowing in the muck of human misery. Beckett struggled more honestly and courageously with the complexities of faith, life, and God than most popular Christian writers today would dare. Thus, I would argue that Beckett is more serious about faith and truth than those believers who only nominally wrestle with mystery. The sad reality is that faith has become a stand-in for certainty. But faith is not certain; it is a risk. And Beckett plumbed the depths while others were content splashing about in the shallows.

Theologians should recognize Beckett as a fellow traveler down the path towards speaking the unspeakable and naming the unnamable. We may not arrive at the same conclusions, but we are indeed on the same path. And that realization has led to this book and the possibility of a theological appreciation of Beckett. Our primary conversation partner will be Jürgen Moltmann, a theologian whose work inspires me to no end. By comparing their different but strikingly similar points of view, I hope to shed new light on Beckett's project—in addition to exploring several vital insights that theology may learn from his work.

Samuel Beckett and Jürgen Moltmann may seem like an unusual pairing, but I know of no two writers better equipped to grapple with the modern world. We will also have reason to discuss Karl Barth, Dietrich Bonhoeffer, Paul Tillich, and the traditions of mystical and apophatic theology. But there are three reasons why Moltmann stands out from the rest.

First, Jürgen Moltmann has radically disrupted the conversation about suffering and God. By challenging the philosophical concept of God's impassibility, his theology offers a unique lens through which we might arrive at a highly original reading of Beckett. The inability to reconcile God's mercy and justice and the problem of a suffering world abandoned by God are both central themes to Beckett's writing. Moltmann's devotion to the suffering of God in Christ and God's solidarity with the God-forsaken will lead to a fascinating reassessment of Beckett's work. The same will be true for Moltmann's unique approach to hope and protest atheism.

Second, a poetic tendency sets Moltmann's work apart from other theologians. We seldom judge theology on its aesthetic qualities, but if a theologian cannot speak eloquently about the God of infinite wonder and beauty, then perhaps they have failed to take their subject seriously. Theology is inherently beautiful, and Moltmann exemplifies how a theologian may speak of God without becoming dry and dull.

Finally, Moltmann and Beckett complement each other because of their shared biography. Both men lived through and were directly involved in the horrors of the Second World War. Moltmann survived the brutal bombings of Hamburg ("Operation Gomorrah"), which killed an estimated 37,000 civilians and desolated the city. After suffering the horrors of the front, he surrendered to the British and spent three years as a prisoner of war. Beckett chose to stay in France—even though his native Ireland was neutral—and volunteered to help with the French resistance, for which he later was awarded the *Croix de Guerre* for bravery. He also worked with the Irish Red Cross in Saint Lô after the war, mostly to return to France, but the experience left its mark (see his poem named after the city). But more substantially, both men not only lived through the horrors of war but forged their unique perspectives in its fires.

Accordingly, both writers would be appropriately called "anti-fascist," as Terry Eagleton has written of Beckett: "If Beckett was a great anti-fascist writer, it is not only because he fought with the French Resistance [...] but because every sentence of his writing keeps faith with powerlessness."[4] Both Moltmann and Beckett display anti-fascism in the traditional political sense. But on a more fundamental level, it is their acute sensitivity to and preference for the powerless, poor, weak, diseased, suffering, and forgotten—or in Biblical terms, their attention to the "least of these"—which makes them great anti-fascist writers. Fascism involves a fixation on strength and power. So the artistic and theological attentiveness Beckett and Moltmann show to the vulnerable and powerless goes a long way in challenging the fascist perspective.

I do not mean to imply that Beckett and Moltmann see eye to eye on everything. Far from it. What makes studying them so interesting is how these two very different writers can share so many convictions and impulses while coming to such radically divergent conclusions. Beckett is no theologian. Nor will this book try to make him into one. I have no illusions of theological *harmony* with Samuel Beckett. I do not think he was as systematic as his critics believe. As he warned, "The danger is in the neatness of identifications."[5] Instead, this book aims to *appreciate* Beckett theologically. Accordingly, I aim to let Beckett remain as he is, "mess" and all, without trying to jam him into a neat theological box.

We will examine four theologically potent themes in Beckett's work. These are not necessarily the only themes, nor are they the most important in Beckett, but I consider them vital for our purpose. The four themes are *suffering, protest, quest,* and *hope.* Here the theological overtones are both fascinating and insightful, but this conversation is not one-sided. We are not merely looking at Beckett from a theological perspective, but the goal is also to see theology in a new light. As a result, the "theology of glory" may give way to a theology of the cross.[6] The theology of strength and success may give way to a theology of weakness and failure. Beckett's quest is ours, and the sooner we realize that, the sooner we will become faithful stewards of the mystery of all mysteries: God.

Theology is at its best when it is honest about the uncertainties we face and the vastness of life's mystery. We often forget that our subject is *God*, the unnamable beyond. We have become complacent and comfortable, domesticating God in the process. As Kierkegaard reflected, "The fundamental error of modern times lies in the fact that the yawning abyss of quality in the difference between God and man has been removed. The result in dogmatic theology is a mockery of God."[7] This analysis rings true still today. And while we may not feel quite as rigidly bound to Kierkegaard's dualism, we would do well to remember that Beckett's path into the "yawning abyss" is also ours. We live in a world of uncertainty; we are thrown mercilessly into the chaos of existence without a map or guide, even if we pretend otherwise. We should not ignore Beckett's struggle with the truth. There is much to appreciate and learn from the depth of his courage and the strength of his resilience in the face of the unnamable.

Culturally, with the rising popularity of Christian fundamentalism and other forms of extremism, Beckett's work has the potential to cure our addiction to certainty. Faith and theology are not safe endeavors; to believe God is to struggle with God for the sake of God, to wrestle like Jacob, lament like Job, and doubt like Thomas. Ethically, Beckett's unwavering fixation on the poor and weak should evoke empathy, humanity, and a hunger for justice in us. In other words, reading Beckett has the potential of making us into more humane humans, theological theologians, and hopeful skeptics; to go on with courage and hope when all seems bleak and hopeless; to refuse to settle for cheap faith. Together with God and against God, we struggle on and on with our wounds.

Nothingness in words enclose

This book does not require expertise in Beckett. However, it will be helpful to have a basic grasp of the unique style of literature he innovated and perfected, which he referred to as the literature of the "unword" in

1937.[8] An early poem from the addenda of *Watt* elegantly introduces two themes that I think set Beckett apart as a writer:

> who may tell the tale
> of the old man?
> weigh absence in a scale?
> mete want with a span?
> the sum assess
> of the world's woes?
> nothingness
> in words enclose?[9]

The final four lines are especially apt. Beckett's literary motivations often gravitate around these two points: assessing the world's woes and enclosing nothingness in words. His obsession with suffering and failure has established the common perception that he is a bleak writer, but that in itself is not necessarily what makes his work difficult. It is rather his striving to name the unnamable and express the inexpressible.

The mature Beckett rejected his friend James Joyce's compulsion to produce erudite, convoluted, intellectually flaunting prose, and instead, he embraced the literature of weakness, impotence, and ignorance. The early Beckett, however, seemed eager to mimic Joyce. *More Pricks than Kicks,* the poem "Whoroscope," and *Dream of Fair to Middling Women* are characterized by an omnipotent, punning, polyglot narrator. His sentences were full of obscure allusions and challenging vocabulary. But then, in 1946, at the beginning of Beckett's most extraordinarily creative period, in which he wrote *Godot* and the novel "trilogy," a revelation shifted his perspective. Anthony Cronin recounts it well:

> Up to this point he had, like others, struggled to be knowing; indeed the 'knowingness' of his early writings is one of their most obvious characteristics. And besides this attempt at knowledgeability, there had been the struggle to do what the novelist is expected to do, to describe a world which would be a realistic simulacrum of the world about him. [...] But according to the revelation that he now had, instead of writing about that exterior world he should have written about the inner world, with its darkness, its ignorance, its uncertainty.[10]

Instead of treading the familiar path of knowing more and portraying the external world of things and events, Beckett chose instead to carve a new path into the self, to uncover the ignorance and doubt at the core of our shared humanity. Because what binds us together is not our strength or intelligence but weakness and ignorance; before a boundless mystery, we are all one. His work relentlessly interrogates existence in all its frailty. As Jonathan Boulter writes, "Beckett's work, at times seemingly so strange, seemingly inhuman, is only ever a compassionate attempt to comprehend humanity itself."[11] He peels back the layers of respectability with which we mask ourselves and gets to the heart of what it is to be human.

Samuel Beckett was many things, but perhaps above all else, he was an artist. And in his eyes, to endeavor down that impossible road is to fail. But that is also the point. Writing about one of his favorite painters, Beckett declared: "To be an artist is to fail, as no other dare fail."[12] That involves an escape from "the field of the possible" and the "plane of the feasible." But then, what possibilities remain? He continues, "Logically none. Yet I speak of an art turning from it in disgust, weary of puny exploits, weary of pretending to be able, of being able, of doing little better than the same old thing, of going a little further along a dreary road."[13] Beckett's art strives persistently onward to "unspeakable home,"[14] to the expression of the inexpressible. This impulse also explains his dedication to weakness and impotence. It is not nihilistic but rather an act of supreme courage, the courage to confront the uncertainties of existence. As Beckett himself explained, "I realised that my own way was in impoverishment, in lack of knowledge and in taking away, subtracting rather than adding."[15] Here art becomes more than just beautiful words—though his work is undoubtedly beautiful. Here art is an act of radical courage.

James Knowlson further explains Beckett's fidelity to failure:

> Writing was for him, he said, a question of 'getting down below the surface' toward what he described as 'the authentic weakness of being.' This was associated with a strong sense of the inadequacy of words to explore the forms of being. 'Whatever is said is so far from the experience'; 'if you really get down to the disaster, the slightest eloquence becomes unbearable.' In this he was far removed, he maintained, from

> the approach of James Joyce: 'Joyce believed in words. All you had to do was rearrange them and they would express what you want.' Beckett never seems to have believed that this was achievable.[16]

In many ways, Beckett's literary quest parallels the iconoclastic development of modern art in the nineteenth and twentieth centuries. The bedrock of artistic expression was once its ability to correspond to reality faithfully. Modern painting, however, began to break its ties with the real and attempted to express the unreal, the inexpressible. That is clear in the works of great artists like Van Gogh, Picasso, Kandinsky, Pollock, Rothko, Bacon, and Beckett's favorites: Bram van Velde and Jack Butler Yeats. Music, too, made this leap. As John Cage once declared, "I have nothing to say, and I am saying it."[17] But literature remained trapped in the belief —false, according to Beckett—that words may adequately express reality. But what if literary realism is a false start?

The endless mysteries of consciousness and being are too vast for words. Our inner life is a hidden, inexpressible mystery, strange even unto ourselves, and our only hope is to strive to express but fail. Indeed, we all strive to speak the unspeakable, every day attempting to say what we think and who we are, knowing all the while we cannot. Beckett's art strives to say the things we *feel* but cannot express, having no words or images or gestures. Yet we must express them somehow. Thus, he aimed to free literature from the tyranny of words, with words. That is why his writing is so radically iconoclastic. For Beckett, the novel is impossible, and thus he unveils the impossibility of writing with writing. As Oliver de Magny explained, "His novels dress the impossibility of the novel in the tattered remains of the novel; his writing becomes a dizzying transparency which both reveals the impossibility of writing and couples it with the writing itself."[18] That is the paradox of his work, and it is what makes reading him so challenging.

Thus, Beckett's fidelity to failure rests on the conviction that accurate representation is impossible. We must speak but cannot. To write is to strive after an impossible, unnamable word. As his *Texts for Nothing* consider, "With what words shall I name my unnamable words?"[19] Words are inadequate. Yet, we are obligated to express reality with words. Beckett's art, then, boils down to this:

> The expression that there is nothing to express, nothing with which to express, nothing from which to express, no power to express, no desire to express, together with the obligation to express.[20]

Beckett was not a philosopher, even though his themes are inherently philosophical. He admitted, "I wouldn't have had any reason to write my novels if I could have expressed their subject in philosophic terms."[21] His work goes *beyond* philosophy; he does not aim merely to understand the human predicament but to try to express those inexpressible facets of human nature, yet to necessarily fail to do so. He tried to speak silence and express in words the inexpressible, "nothingness in words enclose." Beckett was undoubtedly a brilliant, well-read, learned man. Nevertheless, he knew enough to know the limits of understanding. And he sought that which lies beyond knowing, whether silence or nothingness or something else entirely. Words are too blunt of an instrument for the delicate work of expressing the truth. To convey in words what is beyond words, speak the unspeakable, and express the inexpressible—that was Beckett's aim. It is a quest that necessarily leads to failure, but it is the only real path we have; all else is a flight to fantasy.

Lawrence Harvey explains the dilemma well:

> In conversations in 1961 he spoke of writing as a 'groping in the dark,' an enterprise that required the writer to 'see with his fingers.' We find, then, at the heart of Beckett's artistic credo, a correspondence between the intellectual darkness in which man is doomed to live and the irrational organization of words imposed upon the serious artist who wants to say something valid about the conditions of human existence.[22]

A potential parallel may be instructive here between Beckett and the ancient Chinese text known as Zhuangzi. Consider one of the text's most distinctive sayings: "A trap is for fish: when you've got the fish, you can forget the trap. A snare is for rabbits: when you've got the rabbit, you can forget the snare. Words are for meaning: when you've got the meaning, you can forget the words. Where can I find someone who's forgotten words so I can have a word with him?" Although there is no evidence (to my knowledge) of Beckett reading the Zhuangzi text, the comparison is enlightening. Consider a shorter example: "To let understanding stop at what cannot be understood is a high attainment." Thus, there is precedent for Beckett's literary fidelity to failure and the attempt to express the inexpressible. By acknowledging the limits of knowledge and expression, Beckett's literary quest for the unnamable is akin to a spiritual search for the divine. His more direct usage of Christian mysticism, which we will return to in chapter three, echoes this point. These traditions all share with Beckett a sense of striving to transcend the plane of the feasible and fail as none dare fail before.

Finally, besides these philosophical and theological impulses, what else strives to say what cannot be said? In a word, *feeling*. I do not want to be overly reductionistic here, but we can, and perhaps must, read Beckett as an emotional writer who strived to put into words the deepest longings and pains at the core of our shared humanity. Beckett even declared essentially that about his work, "I'm no intellectual. All I am is feeling. 'Molloy' and the others came to me the day I became aware of my own folly. Only then did I begin to write the things I feel."[23] We are thus obligated to try and read him less intellectually and more emotionally. That, of course, does not deny that his work is sophisticated and fascinating, but that is not necessarily the main point. Whenever I read the closing lines from one of Beckett's final pieces, *Stirring Still*, I have a good sense of what it is about: "No matter how no matter where. Time and grief and self so-called. Oh all to end."[24] It is a beautiful lament which at once hopes for and regrets death as the unpredictable yet imminent end we all must face. But we miss the full effect if this is reduced to a purely intellectual declaration. Instead, these words strive to go beyond the feasible and speak the unspeakable, to express that haunting loneliness and suffocating fear at the bottom of our shared humanity. It is this depth of feeling that makes Beckett one of the greatest writers to have ever lived.

COVID-19

As I began the long process of editing this book, the world was brought to its knees by the COVID-19 pandemic. Millions are infected, many thousands have already died, and the death toll is rising daily. In times like these, our cultural naïveté shatters. We pretend our post-enlightenment illusions of a rationalized certainty are unshakable, that we are beyond such primitive, unexplainable catastrophes. We live as if the world owes us an explanation for everything. But there is no app for this, and our frantic Google searches have come up empty. We once accepted the delusional idea that we are in control, that we can achieve a relative degree of certainty, that the world makes sense. It must! Right? But then suddenly it doesn't.

We are drowning in information but starving for wisdom. That much is becoming more apparent every day as this pandemic goes on. We need thinkers who take us beyond cheap certainties, bargain truths, and simplistic rationalities, thinkers who challenge our core assumptions and refuse to accept the easy way out.

We need the wisdom of Job and Ecclesiastes. And Beckett and Moltmann. We do not need another self-help, knowledge-distributer—as if more information ever saved anyone. We need honest wrestling with the truth, an ally in the courageous struggle with mystery and doubt. We need to give up our death-grip on knowledge and certainty and embrace ignorance. But most of all, we need a brother in the dark, crawling on together through the mud and muck. We do not need a God who sits aloof and indifferent up in heaven, but the God who shares our burdens and enters our hells. We need a crucified God.

The world feels God-forsaken. But even in God-forsakenness, we are not alone. As Moltmann argues, God has entered every God-forsaken space in the death of Christ. Beckett, too, writes of these God-forsaken spaces, and when we read his words, we feel less alone. I do not know how I could cope with such a dark horizon if it were not for the courageous words these writers have written.

I do not know if I will survive this pandemic. Nor do I have any guarantees that my family and friends will. I do not know how long it will go on or how many lives it will destroy. No one does. And I cannot shake that haunting image of dying so miserably alone on a quarantined hospital bed hooked up to an inhuman machine, denied the last goodbyes of loved ones. It is not beyond the realm of possibility. Nothing is anymore. Uncertainty has been thrust upon the world like a violent storm. But was it ever really absent? Or have we not merely played this familiar game of distracting ourselves, refusing to face reality by habitually entertaining endless, meaningless trivialities? A plethora of bleak and hopeless possibilities have suddenly forced themselves into our awareness. In these times, the questions we would rather ignore become unavoidable, questions of God, suffering, meaning, and life itself. We cannot flee from reality any longer. After this pandemic, we may try to forget and go back to normal life, that is, to a distracted and numbed life. But we should decide to be courageous instead. Let us face reality in all its uncertainty unflinchingly. If courage is the path we choose, then we may find comfort and strength in the words of Samuel Beckett and Jürgen Moltmann.

1. HE LEAVES NO MAGGOT LONELY

SUFFERING AND SOLIDARITY

There is no literary experience as uniquely moving and disturbing as reading Samuel Beckett. At once strange and familiar, his work brings us face to face with the bleeding heart of humanity with unequaled precision and beauty. But the strangeness of his work—"like difficult music heard for the first time"—means it is often misunderstood. Beckett has been dubbed a bleak, absurd existentialist—even a nihilist. Yet, none of these hasty labels get to the heart of his writing and what makes it so powerful. With this book, I want to introduce you to a different Beckett than the one commonly known. Unlike the popular perception, he is not a brooding pessimist. His work may be bleak and dark, but it is not without an inexplicable glimmer of light. Thus, Beckett's work is a testament to humanity's resilience in the most destitute of worlds.

"If there were only darkness," Beckett explained to Tom Driver, "all would be clear. It is because there is not only darkness but also light that our situation becomes inexplicable."[1] That inexplicable light is why only a flawed reading of Beckett's work would lead us to call it nihilistic. No, nihilism is too neat and easy, a false way out. Instead, Beckett courageously confronted the grey inexplicability of life head-on, refusing to accept cheap answers or settle for an abstract philosophical system to explain away mystery.

This courage to confront the inexplicable is why I think Beckett has written the most boldly compassionate account of human suffering, protest, longing, and hope put into words. In the end, Beckett's work, if it can be said to be "about" anything, is about humanity itself—humanity as it is in its mess and confusion. Boundless compassion for our shared condition shines through every page. As Madeleine Renaud realized, "The best way to understand him is to read his works without looking for any philosophy other than a great human compassion."[2] For all the distress his characters suffer, for all the brutal honesty of Beckett's words, there remains an unshakable core of compassion.

After receiving news that the father of his long-time friend, Alan Schneider, had died, Beckett reached out with a moving letter. Its sentiment of shared humanity illustrates my point about Beckett's work as a whole:

> I know your sorrow and I know that for the likes of us there is no ease for the heart to be had from words or reason and that in the very assurance of sorrow's fading there is more sorrow. So I offer you only my deeply affectionate and compassionate thoughts and wish for you only that the strange thing may never fail you, whatever it is, that gives us the strength to live on and on with our wounds.[3]

That final phrase hits home: "To live on and on with our wounds." It captures so well the power of Beckett's art. Together we go on with our pain, accumulated from a life of heartbreak and sadness. Yet we are not alone, and something—or perhaps Someone—is with us and strengthens our resolve to go on.

The more we understand Beckett on his terms, the more difficult it becomes to reconcile him with the common caricatures. As Tom Driver understood, "Beckett's writing had seemed permeated with love for human beings and with a kind of humor that I could reconcile neither with despair nor with nihilism."[4] His work oozes empathy and humanity. While others have stressed his pessimism—of course, no one denies his work is dark, but it is not *only* dark—the work itself expresses a paradoxical hope, courage, and kindness. To read Beckett is to feel the plight of another soul. His characters may repulse us, but we cannot help discovering a bit of ourselves in them. By writing about the literary "least of these," Beckett shows compassion on the lowest and weakest of humanity. Thus, the lowest and weakest parts of ourselves find comfort in a strange hope. We are affirmed in the odd affirmation of Beckett's miserable people. Any writer with half a brain can affirm the best in humanity, but it takes an artist to find beauty in the worst of us.

Beckett has no answers to ease the confusion of this mess called life, no philosophy or dogma to provide a sense of closure or control. That is why he cannot be a nihilist, an existentialist, or even a philosopher in the ordinary sense of the word; their solutions are far too neat and tidy. He is a writer *sui generis,* without precedent or school. An encounter with Beckett means coming face to face with an unrelenting iconoclasm, which is why the unique experience of reading his work is at once terrifying and yet terrifyingly liberating. There is beauty in the destruction of idols. There is anxiety in freedom.

Despite his rejection of dogmatic certainties and systems, he writes a philosophically and theologically drenched literature, unmatched by even some of the best philosophers. There is a unique depth to his pursuit of what is real and honest. He remained *on the way,* perpetually unsatisfied with cheap results. And that may be the ultimate test of a good philosopher—not the depth of their answers but the inexhaustibility of their questions.

But the point of reading Beckett is not to know more. Instead, it is to feel the inexplicable weight of human suffering and hope. Beckett once declared, "I'm not an intellectual. All I am is feeling."[5] His depth of human compassion and the drive to write what is felt rather than what is known is the first element of his work that lends itself to theological appreciation. The themes of suffering and solidarity, both God's and ours, will be highlighted in this chapter, beginning with his best-known work.

Waiting for Godot

In *Waiting for Godot,* as Bert O. States writes, Beckett "converts theology into mythic poetry."[6] Even if that is a slight overstatement, there are far too many convergences in Beckett's great play to ignore; it is drenched in theological themes. But the common question—"Is Godot God?"—should be judged as far too simplistic, not to mention theologically naive. Because in fact, God is nothing like Godot. Simply put: the Christian God is no deus ex machina. In my reading of the play, God is not Godot. Instead, if God is anywhere, God is paradoxically with Gogo, Didi,

Lucky, and Pozzo, waiting and hoping and suffering as they mourn *the absence* of any such deus ex machina. The God revealed in Christ is the suffering God, the God who bears our burdens and joins our miserable plight. God does not save from above in might and strength but from below in solidarity and suffering, not with an abstract power but the power of co-suffering love. Only a faulty theological basis looks for God in Godot. The Christian story is, in many ways, about the destruction of the Godot-idol. As Dietrich Bonhoeffer memorably explained:

> This is the crucial distinction between Christianity and all religions. Human religiosity directs people in need to the power of God in the world, God as deus ex machina. The Bible directs people toward the powerlessness and the suffering of God; only the suffering God can help.[7]

God is not only the One waited for but the One who waits. The cruel, white-bearded, impassible Godot of abstract authority and might, wholly unbothered by the trivial sufferings of pitiful tramps, is nothing like the God revealed in Christ. Hope in the God of Godot is a false hope. It was a hope condemned and put to death as Christ cried out, "My God, why have you forsaken me?" Godot died in the death of Christ precisely because God did not swoop in like a mighty victor to rescue Christ from death, but rather, He bore the brutal end of bitter abandonment and lonely agony. Christ's prayer went unanswered. God saves not with an eleventh-hour display of power but in the weakness of suffering before a silent sky. And while Christian faith confesses that God raised Christ from the dead, that hope is an unnamable hope (as we will see in chapter four), the kind of hope that only exists on the other side of hopelessness. Yes, God raised Christ, but first, Christ suffered and died a God-forsaken death.

Thus, identifying God with Godot distracts from a far more powerful theme: solidarity in suffering, compassion in grief, and fellowship in waiting. In the light of God's co-suffering love, we can arrive at a unique reading of the text that its religious and theological interpreters have so far overlooked.

In a grievously underrated scene, this theme is evident. As Estragon (Gogo) sleeps and suffers from a nightmare, Vladimir (Didi) takes off his coat and lays it across his friend's shoulders to comfort him. Vladimir paces to warm himself as Estragon wakes with a sudden jolt. Vladimir hastens to his side to embrace him, "There... there... Didi is there... don't be afraid."[8] In a destitute world, one man comforts another. The scene is as simple as that. But it is a courageous act of fellowship, and in the bleak world of *Godot*, its light shines with stark clarity against the darkness all around it. The tramps are forgotten by the world; they experience nightly beatings and wait for a word from an unknown Godot, who may never come. The pair have been marginalized and dehumanized so brutally they are not even sure if they exist, "Estragon: We always find something, eh Didi, to give us the impression we exist?"[9] Even hanging themselves from the tree seems like a more exciting option than facing bleak reality. In such a world, Vladimir shows compassion to Estragon; because the world is little else but darkness and despair, this simple act is profoundly spiritual and humane.

The first time Ruby Cohn saw *Waiting for Godot,* her reaction was not intellectual but visceral, rooted in a deep sense of solidarity: "And yet I knew almost at once that those two French-speaking tramps were me; more miserable, more lovable, more humorous, more desperate. But me."[10] The prisoners at San Quentin had the same experience. Martin Esslin writes, "And what had bewildered the sophisticated audiences of Paris, London, and New York was immediately grasped by an audience of convicts."[11] They instinctively knew what the play was about. As one inmate wrote to Beckett, "We are all waiting for Godot and do not know that he is already here. Yes, here. Godot is my neighbour in the cell next to mine. Let us do something to help him then, change the shoes that are hurting him!"[12] Indeed, Beckett's affinity for the incarcerated is a moving testament to his devotion to the poor and downtrodden. His Parisian apartment looked out over *la Santé* prison, and their cries were a constant reminder. He would sometimes even communicate with them by mirror messages in Morse code.[13] All of these points indicate that we will not arrive at a proper reading of *Waiting for Godot* solely through intellectual astuteness. Rather, we must focus on its empathetic vision of shared suffering and thus discover its compassionate core with our hearts.

If we follow this thread further, it may be possible to read the play as a kind of retelling of the Good Samaritan parable (Luke 10:25-37). Rather than a purely moral parable, however, the Good Samaritan story should be understood here as a profound commendation of co-suffering love and the power of solidarity, of bearing each other's burdens as God bears ours. With this in mind, consider the way Didi and Gogo interact with the only other characters in the play: Pozzo and Lucky. Pozzo abuses Lucky, treating him more as an object than a man, and Didi and Gogo express indignation against that injustice: "To treat a man… like that… I think that… no… a human being… no… it's a scandal!"[14] Vladimir even calls Lucky "Such an old and faithful servant," echoing Christ's parable of the sheep and goats (Matthew 25:23).[15] Then in act two, Pozzo is inexplicably blind and depends on Lucky's help to get around. Estragon and Vladimir cry out with a kind of *Kyrie Eleison*, "God have pity on me!"[16] Pozzo, too, cries out for help, and Vladimir shows compassion on him, "Poor Pozzo!"[17] Shortly following these exchanges, Vladimir proclaims a moral call to action that centers around our shared humanity. There are several subtle similarities between this monologue and the Good Samaritan parable, so I quote it at length:

> Let us not waste our time in idle discourse! [*Pause. Vehemently.*] Let us do something, while we have the chance! It is not every day we are needed. Not indeed that we personally are needed. Others would meet the case equally well, if not better. To all mankind they were addressed, those cries for help still ringing in our ears! But at this place, at this moment of time, all mankind is us, whether we like it or not. Let us make the most of it, before it is too late![18]

Christ's parable makes a comparable point. It comes in response to the question, "Who is my neighbor?" Jesus tells of a man beaten, robbed, stripped, and left to die on the road from Jerusalem to Jericho. A priest comes along and ignores his suffering, so does a Levite. They pass to the other side. It is not their problem. But a Samaritan—a despised figure at the time—acts with compassion and helps. He bandages his wounds and pays the expenses for his recovery. In doing so, he makes the man's burdens his own. Jesus concludes, "Which of these three, do you think, was a neighbor to the man who fell into the hands of these robbers?" (Luke 10:36).[19] The man who first asked the question responds, "The one who showed him mercy." So Christ declares, "Go and do likewise." According to the Gospel, that is also how God saves; not by lofty might, like the priest and Levite who imagine themselves above the man, but by joining the plight of the poor, weak, and destitute, by bearing their suffering to the point of death. Only the suffering God can help.

By responding to Pozzo's call for help, Vladimir and Estragon act as Good Samaritans. But as the play makes clear, Pozzo's cry was directed to all humanity. The person who hears and acts to help those who suffer is proven to be their neighbor. The text echoes precisely this point. Pozzo asks if they are friends, and Vladimir concludes, "We've proved we are, by helping him."[20]

This theme continues following the most famous line of the play. Pozzo laments the futility of a life that ends in death: "One day we are born, one day we shall die, the same day, the same second [...] They give birth astride of a grave, the light gleams an instant, then it's night once more."[21] Shortly after, Vladimir meditates on the duty we have to our neighbor: "Was I sleeping, while the others suffered? Am I sleeping now?"[22] It is one thing to reflect on the nature of suffering, and if that is all Beckett did, then his work may live up to its nihilistic perception. But he does not merely revel in the darkness of existence. There is darkness *and* light. The beauty and strength of the light is thus all the more profound because it does not shy away from the darkness.

A theological interpretation of the Good Samaritan parable sees it not merely as an ethical call to be kind to strangers. Instead, it is the pronouncement of God's solidarity with the least of these. As Moltmann writes, "In Christ, God and our neighbour are a unity, and what God has joined together, man shall not put apart, least of all the theologian."[23] God identifies, not with the priest or the Levite, but with the man who was robbed and beaten. God is the suffering victim. It is with this in mind that we should discover God's presence in Beckett's play. God suffers with Vladamir and Estragon as they wait for a deus ex machina that never comes. Yet, it is also relevant to see how this connects theologically to the play's central image: the cross. The crucifixion event is God's unambiguous identification with the poor and weak; God is the brother of all the God-forsaken.

Beckett's play begins as Vladimir reflects on the two thieves crucified with Christ. After a silence, "deep in thought," he recalls: "One of the thieves was saved. It's a reasonable percentage."[24] The account of the two thieves is a crucial allusion. It shapes not only the plot of *Waiting for*

Godot but offers insight into the pathos of the play. Two thieves, like the two tramps, wait for salvation. There is uncertainty about whether one of them was indeed saved, just as the play leaves us with little indication of whether Didi and Gogo will meet Godot. But the crucifixion account has a more profound significance besides establishing the structure of the play.

The centerpiece on stage is the tree. Didi and Gogo wait for Godot at the tree, and the allusion to the cross is clear. The pair even contemplate hanging themselves from the tree, mimicking the well-known theological conclusion of St. Paul, that Christ became a curse for us by hanging on a tree (Galatians 3:13). The tree has no leaves in the first act but inexplicably blooms in the second. Whether this is a symbol of resurrection hope, or even if it serves no real purpose at all, it is hard to ignore the allusions to Christian theology surrounding the tree image.

Another allusion is to the parable of the sheep and goats (Matthew 25:31-46), which takes the same dualistic shape as the two thieves crucified with Christ. It is an eschatological parable that tells of a final separation and judgment of all people, as a shepherd separates sheep from goats. Those on the right inherit the Kingdom of God because they acted justly towards the "least of these," they gave them food and water, welcomed them in as strangers, cared for them, and clothed them. "Truly I tell you," Jesus explains, "just as you did it to one of the least of these who are members of my family, you did it to me" (Matthew 25:40). But on the left, those who did not act justly to the least of these are cast out. The parable shares a similar ethical and theological message as the Good Samaritan, but it goes further by more explicitly identifying God with the "least of these." God is with the hungry, homeless, incarcerated, and poor; the plight of the oppressed is also God's.

Beckett makes several explicit references to the parable of the sheep and goats. The most direct is when a young messenger boy arrives (the first time) to tell Didi and Gogo that Godot will not come today. Vladimir asks the boy what he does, and we learn that he tends to the goats while his brother tends to the sheep. However, in an interesting reversal, Godot beats the brother who tends to the sheep but not the one who tends to the goats (implying that the goats are saved and the sheep are damned). The boy does not know why Godot does this, which is on par with Didi and Gogo's ignorance of why one thief was saved and the other damned. The wrath of their master seems cruel and arbitrary. In the next chapter, we will discuss Beckett's metaphysical protest. But here, we should note subtle indignation against the sort of God who saves and damns human beings arbitrarily—such as the God of Calvin's "horrible decree," the doctrine of double-predestination. For Beckett, the great sin of humanity is the sin of being born. He alludes to this conviction within the first few pages of the play, but it is repeated often in other works. It would be unjust for God to create human beings as sinners, only then to condemn some and save others aimlessly. Beckett's account of Godot's two sons, as well as Didi and Gogo's musing on the two thieves, highlights the cruelty of such a cosmological arrangement.

In another scene, Vladimir protests that Estragon cannot go barefoot, but Gogo retorts, "Christ did," which sets up the following lines:

> Vladimir: Christ! What has Christ got to do with it? You're not going to compare yourself to Christ!
> Estragon: All my life I've compared myself to him.
> Vladimir: But where he lived it was warm, it was dry!
> Estragon: Yes. And they crucified quick.[25]

Later in the play, Vladimir remarks, "To every man his little cross. [*He sighs.*] Till he dies. [*Afterthought.*] And is forgotten."[26] For Beckett, life is one long crucifixion, but to Christ's benefit, they "crucified quick." Another important example of the cross/tree image is when Vladimir and Estragon decide to "do the tree, for the balance."[27] They hop on one leg like a tree. And Estragon asks, "Do you think God sees me?" Failing to "do the tree," he yells, "at the top of his voice," "God have pity on me!"[28] Thus, their desperate quest for meaning in a God-forsaken world echoes the words of Christ on the cross, "My God, my God, why have you forsaken me?"

Finally, near the end of the play, after being told yet again that Godot will not come today, Vladimir and Estragon give serious attention to the tree—almost as if they had not seen it before and are just now seeing it for what it is. It feels like a moment of religious solemnity. "Vladimir: [*Silence. He looks at the tree.*] Everything's dead but the tree. Estragon:

[*looking at the tree*] What is it? Vladimir: It's the tree."[29] Notably, he does not reply, "It's *a* tree," but rather, "It's *the* tree." Throughout the play, it is only referred to as *the* tree. With the prevalence of the tree/cross image, it seems too intentional not to refer to Christ's cross. It is also noteworthy that the play ends where it began: they contemplate hanging themselves from the tree. "We'll hang ourselves tomorrow. [*Pause.*] Unless Godot comes."[30]

Essential to the play is Beckett's conviction that every human life is like a crucifixion event. Beckett has no sense of Jesus as divine, but Christ's suffering is, for him, a symbol of humanity as a whole. We suffer before an indifferent, silent sky, without meaning, direction, or consolation. And this is where my reading of the play comes to a point. *Waiting for Godot* expresses, in miniature, the story of all humanity. But it is also the story of Good Friday. As Christ suffered and died abandoned by God, forsaken by friends, and alone in His agony—so we all suffer and die in this God-forsaken world. Christ is no more a savior than anyone else, for Beckett, and His death exemplifies every human death.

But in suffering, there is the strange, inexplicable comfort of knowing we are not alone. Schopenhauer thought we should greet one another on the street as "fellow sufferers" rather than "sir" or "madam." Upon realizing our common humanity, we must see every person we meet as taking part in universally shared agony. To be human is to suffer, and this realization gives us both courage and compassion: the courage to face the darkness and go on in spite of it, and the compassion to be tender towards the plight of our neighbor.

In suffering, there is solidarity. We are joined together in our shared sorrows. Yet, there is not only darkness but glimmers of hope, and that is what makes life inexplicable. It is a constant source of hope—that we share each other's burdens. And this strange hope persists throughout Beckett's play. It is a resilient hope against hope. The darkness is unbearably bleak, but we are not alone. Theologically, it is into this same darkness that Christ became one with us; from the stable to the cross, Christ bore our suffering as His own. Christ, too, waits for Godot, for salvation. Christ waits and suffers with us.

God is not Godot. The God of the Bible is no authoritarian tyrant, but the God who suffers with the suffering and waits with those who wait. If God is in *Waiting for Godot,* God is with the lonely tramps who wait aimlessly and suffer hopelessly. God is no deus ex machina. Christ shattered that idol on the cross. Godot is dead, but Christ suffers and waits with us in the bitter shadow of Godot's absence.

To live on and on with our wounds

Beckett's friend and fellow playwright, Harold Pinter, penned one of my favorite descriptions of his work, which identifies so well the beauty and power of Beckett's art:

> The farther he goes the more good it does me. I don't want philosophies, tracts, dogmas, creeds, way outs, truths, answers, *nothing from the bargain basement.* He is the most courageous, remorseless writer going and the more he grinds my nose in the shit the more I am grateful to him. He's not fucking me about, he's not leading me up any garden, he's not slipping me any wink, he's not flogging me a remedy or a path or a revelation or a basinful of breadcrumbs, he's not selling me anything I don't want to buy, he doesn't give a bullock whether I buy or not, *he hasn't got his hand over his heart.* Well, I'll buy his goods, hook, line and sinker, because he leaves no stone unturned and no maggot lonely. He brings forth a body of beauty. His work is beautiful.[31]

It is better to have our noses rubbed "in the shit" of life than to pretend it does not exist, to distract ourselves to death from it. This realization is at once one of profound hope and compassion. Life ends, and that is its terror, but life *is* and must be embraced as such. We cannot have it on any other terms. Beckett never gives us an easy way out, but he leaves no maggot lonely in the process.

That is a lesson Christians have not been quick enough to learn, even though our tradition is rich with examples to the contrary. Modern-day Christian faith is cheap and compromised by its refusal to face up to the brute realities of suffering and death—especially American "health and wealth" Christianity, which identifies empty positivity with God. Cheap optimism and the idea that God guarantees a positive outcome to life is a lie and fundamentally incongruent with the cross of Christ. The cross alone distinguishes the Christian faith from the projection of our empty, egotistical desires under the banner of faith.[32] But true faith is trust *in spite of* doubt, in spite of the darkness around us, and *not* the denial of doubt and darkness.

Christian faith embraces the brute realism of death because it embraces the realism of Christ's cross. Indeed, we may try to run from our distress and ignore the absurd brevity of life, but we would only be running from life itself, ultimately deluding ourselves into throwing more of it away. Our desire to escape the darkness of the present life is a denial of life itself. But this is not a new idea: it is as old as the books of Ecclesiastes and Job. It is present in the often neglected tradition to meditate on death's inevitability, *momento mori.* In the nineteenth century, Kierkegaard challenged us to embrace the absurdities we so often try to suppress. We can never escape the brute realities of human finitude. We will either fill our lives with meaningless distractions or embrace our limitations and reconcile ourselves with the absurdity of existence. Indeed, "They give birth astride of a grave." Or as Ecclesiastes declared, "Merest breath, said Qohelet, merest breath. All is mere breath."[33]

Another beautiful description of Beckett's writing comes from the actress Lisa Dawn. On his unflinching dedication to the big questions of existence, she remarked, "What I love about Beckett [is] he doesn't try to tidy them off. There's nothing to sell here, you know, he's not offering a polemic or a P.R., or a story to entertain us. He's simply standing there in all of his confusion [...] *putting his hand on the wound.*"[34] Beckett never tries to resolve life's tensions. He stands with us in all the mess and chaos of existence and puts a hand over the wound. It is an open wound, and there is little chance it will heal, but what a great comfort it is to know we are not alone.

It is here that the theological parallels become profound. Beckett not only stands in the tradition of Job and Ecclesiastes, but his work lends itself to the theology of God's co-suffering love. Modern theologians have begun questioning the old doctrine of divine impassibility, that God stands aloof to human misery and pain. Jürgen Moltmann has prominently stressed the suffering of God, that God became weak and vulnerable in Jesus Christ. God not only put a hand over the wound but entered the mess of existence and has taken up our suffering plight as God's own. The God of the Bible became a man and bore our sin and alienation to the point of death upon a cross. Life may be full to the brink of suffering and sorrow, but God is with us and bears our burdens.

Yet God is not only *in* suffering, but suffering is *in* God, as the divine Trinitarian life opens up to embrace the bleeding heart of humanity. Our God is the crucified God. As Moltmann writes, "The death of the Son of God on the cross reaches deep into the nature of God and, above all other meanings, is an event which takes place in the innermost nature of God himself."[35] The cross was an event at the very heart of the Triune God; God defines Godself as the crucified God of boundless co-suffering love.

Karl Barth's theology hinged on the conviction, "Who God is and what it is to be divine is something we have to learn where God has revealed Himself and His nature."[36] To this, Eberhard Jüngel comments: "No concept of God arrived at independent of the reality of Jesus Christ may decide what is possible and impossible for God. Rather, we are to say from what God as man in Christ is, does and suffers: 'God can do this.'"[37] This logic establishes the basis for Moltmann's challenge to the doctrine of divine impassibility, and it is how he can assert that God suffers with humanity, taking our suffering into God's innermost Self. God can and does suffer with us because, in Christ, God suffered. The cross is normative for the doctrine of God.

Thus, the only Christian response to the problem of suffering is to affirm that "God was in Christ." That is not an answer to the open wound of misery but gives us the courage to go on in spite of it. As Moltmann writes, "It is the real task of faith and theology to make it possible for us to survive, to go on living, with this open wound."[38] God suffered and suffers with us still because God entered into our plight, taking up human misery as God's own, sharing our distress, and dying on a God-forsaken cross. It is not out of any deficiency of God's being, but rather, out of the greatness of God's love that God suffers.[39]

The old philosophers and theologians posited God's impassability to defend the very Godness of God. To be God, in their mind, was to be perfect. And if God is perfect, God cannot change or be changed by anything or anyone, even God. So it was logically necessary to conclude that God cannot suffer passion because to do so would be to experience change. But such a God is an idol. The Christian God is not a God of abstract perfection—especially when we think we know the right definition of perfection and apply our *human* definitions onto God. Instead, the Christian God is the God of love because this is the God revealed in

Jesus Christ. Love, not perfection, is the chief attribute of the Christian doctrine of God.

Moltmann explains all this well in an apt summary:

> When the crucified Jesus is called the 'image of the invisible God', the meaning is that *this* is God, and God is like *this*. God is not greater than he is in this humiliation. God is not more glorious than he is in this self-surrender. God is not more powerful than he is in this helplessness. God is not more divine than he is in this humanity. The nucleus of everything that Christian theology says about 'God' is to be found in this Christ event. The Christ event on the cross is a God event.[40]

God suffered in Christ and suffers with us still in our misery and death. God was most God-like on the cross when humanity's suffering was brought into the very Trinitarian life and love of God. It is not a contradiction of God's perfection to say that God suffers—but its completion. God suffers *because* God is perfect love. God entered a God-forsaken world and penetrated the heart of our darkness and despair. When Christ cried out, "My God, why have you forsaken me?" he reached the heart of the human condition. There God became the God of the God-forsaken, our brother in the absence of God.

With Beckett's play in mind, we must theologically say that Christ, too, waits for Godot. In our misery, God is present in the absence of God, as God waits with us for the glorification of all things in the new heaven and earth. The tree image that is so important to Beckett's play is also the symbol of God's unfailing solidarity with human suffering. God suffers with us so that we might one day enjoy with God the glory of the new creation. For Moltmann, God is not already in paradise without us. God, too, waits for the new creation of all things and the final glorification of God. God waits with humanity for the coming of God, the consummation of all things. God waits for Godot.

Beckett does not have this point in mind, of course, but I cannot help myself from seeing the parallels. If human history is a cross and wait, as Beckett implies in his work, then theologically speaking, he is correct. But we must add, in the God-forsaken space in which Gogo and Didi wait, God waits with us and suffers what we suffer. Their open wound is also God's. If life is one long Good Friday, then God is with us in the midst of it all. And the Christian faith professes hope in the redemption of all things precisely because God is with us in the depths of human misery. Because Christ descended into hell, no hell is untouched by God's co-suffering love.

If human suffering is an open wound, then it is also *God's wound.* The traditional question of theodicy, of why God allows or causes suffering, is unanswerable. Moltmann recognized this. He does not claim to overcome the classic problem of evil, but he does challenge how we think of God in suffering.[41] God is not indifferent to human pain. Instead, our wound is God's wound. To use Pinter's phrase, *God leaves no maggot lonely.* God waits with us, goes ahead of us, and prepares the way for a day in which justice and mercy will reign, suffering will be no more, and all things will be made new. God will answer for evil one day, but God waits with us and shares our wounds until that day.

It is from this vantage point that we can appreciate Beckett's fixation on suffering and death. He plumbs the depths of human misery and distress, but it is not a world totally without hope. By rubbing our noses in the mess of existence, Beckett brings us to the foot of the cross, the cross of human suffering. But he also brings us to the foot of God's cross, to the suffering of God.

Endgame

Another of Beckett's theatrical masterpieces, *Endgame,* continues his obsession with the image of the cross and the literary expression of God-forsaken spaces. The very first line of the play, which echoes throughout the work, is an allusion to the crucifixion: "Finished, it's finished, nearly finished, it must be nearly finished."[42] Recall Christ's words on the cross, "It is finished" (John 19:30). But this is only the beginning. *Endgame* is arguably Beckett's most God-haunted play, overflowing with allusions not only to the cross but the end of the world.

The general sense pervading the play is that the world is at its endgame, a term borrowed from chess (another of Beckett's life-long obsessions) to indicate the final acts of human misery before an inevitable end. This term also gives the play strong eschatological overtones. Beckett once explained that Hamm is in a losing position from the beginning, yet he plays on like a bad chess player refusing to concede defeat, "Me to play." As the play laments, echoing not only Hamm's position but that of all human life in which death is inevitable, "The end is in the beginning and yet you go on."[43] Death and suffering are foregone conclusions, but we go on regardless.

The play's atmosphere is of a universal Good Friday, the last gasps of human existence, with an eschatological sense of finality pervading each image. Hamm begins and ends with a red cloth covering his face, resembling the Veil of Veronica, which was, according to the Catholic tradition, used to wipe Christ's bloody face on the road to the cross. The character's names hint towards the cross image as well. Hamm is truncated from "hammer," and every other character alludes to some form of "nail." Clov resembles the French "*clou,*" Nagg the German "*Nagel,*" and Nell sounds like nail when spoken aloud. Thus, on stage, the three nails are driven by an immobile Hamm-er ever onward to greater misery, like the three nails that went through the hands and feet of Christ. Beckett considered placing a Bible front and center on the stage in an early version of the play, but it would have been redundant given the abundance of Biblical allusions.

References to Noah and the flood heighten the eschatological sense of humanity's end. The names Nagg and Hamm are a play on Noah and Ham. The flood was a global catastrophe, and the play hints that the world has met a similar end. They take shelter in a suffocating room just like those who escaped the wrath of God in the ark. They are the final remnant of humanity. Hamm proclaims, "You stink already. The whole place stinks of corpses." But Clov adds, "The whole universe."[44] This gives us a sense of the play existing in a post-apocalyptic world.

The book of Revelation's imagery is frequently alluded to with dualistic refrains such as light and dark, earth and sea, life and death, beginning and end. But there are also explicit allusions to the last judgment and the resurrection of the dead. At one point, Clov tests an alarm clock and comments on how loud it rings: "Fit to wake the dead!"[45] In the original French, this line is more explicit, "Worthy of the Last Judgment." Shortly after, Clov asks Hamm, "Do you believe in the life to come?"[46] The possibility of a new beginning was also the message of Noah and the flood in Genesis: a new world from the old. Hamm's passing reference to Daniel's *mene mene teqal ufarsin*, written on the walls at Belshazzar's feast, only reinforces the play's emphasis on an imminent end, "God has numbered the days of your kingdom and brought it to an end" (Daniel 5:26).[47]

Hamm humorously plays with one of Christ's famous commands, "Get out of here and love one another! Lick your neighbor as yourself!"[48] This remark follows a crucial but broken memory he struggles to recount. It is fragmented and hard to decipher, but it seems that Hamm, before the world's unnamed catastrophic end, was a wealthy man of means. He recalls a bitterly cold Christmas Eve. A beggar approached him, crawling on the ground, his face covered in dirt and tears. Hamm says not to look at him, that he is a busy man. The man begs him to take his little one, a little boy. The beggar cannot take care of him and will soon be dead. Or at least, he pleas can Hamm spare a piece of bread. Hamm refuses his dying request and mockingly adds, "But what in God's name do you imagine? [...] That there's manna in heaven still for imbeciles like you?"[49] The man had crawled for three days to ask for help. He again implores Hamm to take the child. Hamm trails off and does not conclude the memory, though it is apparent that he has not helped the boy. That leads to a sobering reflection, "All those I might have helped."[50] Although, Hamm quickly doubts he could have been much help. Given the totality of the catastrophe and the state the world is in, no one could have been helped. But he remains haunted by his failure to live up to Christ's words, and so he mocks them bitterly.

The play also alludes to the eschatological parable of the Ten Virgins. There were ten virgins, five wise and five foolish, who wait for the bridegroom's arrival. The foolish virgins eventually run out of oil for their lamps, but the wise brought extra. When the bridegroom arrives, the five wise virgins enter the house of their master, but the five foolish ones are cast out into the darkness. In Beckett's text, Clov says to Hamm, critically, "When old Mother Pegg asked you for oil for her lamp and you told her to get out to hell, you know what was happening then, no? [*Pause.*] You know what she died of, Mother Pegg? Of darkness."[51] Hamm tries to defend himself and claims he did not have any oil, but Clov knows he did.

Finally, in a scene that Beckett considered vital, Hamm and Clov try to pray the Lord's Prayer. The play was initially banned in London and Ireland because of this scene. Hamm exclaims, after a failed attempt at praying: "The bastard! He doesn't exist!"[52] Beckett was pressured to change the line but refused. In a letter to George Devine, he compared this "indispensable line" to another, famous example: "It is no more blasphemous than 'My God, my God, why hast Thou forsaken me?'"[53] Like Christ's cry from the cross, Hamm's lament is a bitter, last-ditch plea before the silence of God. The themes we have explored so far all culminate in this paradoxical insult. The absence of God haunts the play, even though the text overflows with religious and theological imagery. But the greatest sin God commits is that God does not exist. God has abandoned the world at its end, and so the game is lost from the start. It is no wonder why Beckett called this play bleaker and more inhumane than *Godot.* Yet it is precisely here, in this God-forsaken space, that the paradoxical presence of God is apparent. As Moltmann writes, "There is no 'outside the gate' with God, if God himself is the one who died outside the gate on Golgotha for those who are outside."[54] Our bleak God-forsaken spaces have been embraced and included in the very life and light of the Triune God.

But *Endgame* is not a story of total darkness. In the end, Clov sets out to leave Hamm after seeing faintly from the window a young boy. Yet, the play ends in a stalemate. It is uncertain whether or not Clov leaves. He feels bound still to the doomed, dying, immobile Hamm but pulled on by the hope of new life. He is like the wretched man Paul describes in Romans 7. He is tied to the old yet pulled on by the new, paradoxically dead and dying yet alive.

Suffering abounds at the end of the world. In a line that Beckett once said was his favorite, Hamm asks what Nagg is doing. "Clov: He's crying. Hamm: Then he's living."[55] But as much as Beckett enjoyed the dark humor of such a line, he considered Nell's the most important: "Nothing is funnier than unhappiness."[56] There remains a gleam of humor in such a tragic play. But what I find fascinating about both lines is how they indicate Beckett's attentiveness to unhappiness. Unlike some playwrights, it is not his character's joy that matters but their sorrows. His compassion for the plight of suffering humanity is apparent with this. Beckett's work invokes empathy for human misery. But we must not overlook the humor. As Tom Driver realized, his comedy is a sign of courage, not despair:

> Beckett himself, or so I take it, has repented of the desire for certainty.

> There are therefore released in him qualities of affirmation that his interpreters often miss. That is why the laughter of his plays is warm, his concern for his characters affectionate. His warm humor and affection are not the attributes of defeatism but the consequences of what Paul Tillich has called 'the courage to be.'[57]

The question *Endgame* implicitly asks is, "Where is God at the end of the world?" Theologically speaking, God is in the midst of the frail and weak; God is with those who struggle to pray but cannot, who feel the suffocating weight of God-forsakenness, who breathe their last in the trash heaps of humanity. The cross is central to Beckett's vision of the tragedy of human existence: life is brief, absurd, and haunted by the absence of God and meaning. But the play is also very funny, and there is absurd compassion in even the most destitute slices of reality. Yet God is present in the God-forsaken spaces. The cross proclaims God's unwavering will to be our God, God for us and with us, even in the pit of hell. Even at our endgame, cosmically or existentially, God is with us. This realization gives us unshakable courage to go on in spite of being unable to.

"Dante and the Lobster"

"Dante and the Lobster," from Beckett's collection, *More Pricks Than Kicks,* overflows with cruciform images. It is one of Beckett's most successful short stories, although it still bears his early tendency to obscure the mundane. The main character, Belacqua—based on a character from Dante—reads Dante, sacramentally prepares lunch, buys cheese and a lobster, attends an Italian lesson, and finally ends up at his aunt's house to cook the lobster. The grocer who sells him his Gorgonzola cheese is like the figure Pilate (though he does not wash his hands), but he also morphs into a figure like Christ (throwing his arms out cruciform). Throughout the text, Belacqua contemplates the impending execution of a man named McCabe, sitting in his cell awaiting death. Thus, Beckett transforms the mundane acts of studying and shopping into a Christ-drenched icon of suffering.

The central theme of the story, according to Ruby Cohn, is "the impossibility of reconciling divine justice and mercy in this world."[58]

Beckett protests against injustice and the indifference of God. But theologically speaking, such a protest against God is holy iconoclasm. It is a protest against the idol of an impassible deity. Thus, God is not the object of Beckett's protest but its subject and motivating force. God, too, protests against such a God.

Cohn provides helpful insight for understanding the McCabe account, which Belacqua contemplates throughout the story.[59] Linguistically, McCabe's name is a sonic mix of Cain and Abel—whom Belacqua also references in the text—thus symbolizing both murderer and victim in one, a prototype for all humanity. Historically, McCabe was convicted of six counts of murder and, in the story, is set to hang at dawn. It is this upcoming event that sparks Belacqua to contemplate the irreconcilability of justice and mercy. The real McCabe was executed on December 9, 1926, while Beckett was a Trinity College student. McCabe protested his innocence until the very end, but he was hanged because of a single testimony. No pardon was given, which, in the story, strikes Belacqua as inhumane. The real execution likely made a similar impression on the young Beckett.

The McCabe account is vital to the story, but it often sits below the surface. Thematically, it parallels the story's climactic conclusion, which is also one of Beckett's most memorable endings. Throughout the story, Belacqua was unaware of the lobster alive in his bag. He did not know they must be boiled alive. He is taken aback by the horror of such a death but comforts himself with the thought that it will be quick. The final sentence cuts in with an omnipresent narrator who offers a stark, brutal correction:

> Well, thought Belacqua, it's a quick death, God help us all.
>
> *It is not.*[60]

Beckett links Christ on the cross and McCabe in the noose to the death of the lobster. Belacqua explicitly contemplates the theme of justice and mercy immediately before boiling the poor creature. He asks, "Why not piety and pity both [...]? Why not mercy and Godliness together?"[61] He thinks of Jonah and "the gourd and the pity of a jealous God on Nineveh." And feels compassion for "poor McCabe." He steps out of himself and empathizes with McCabe, trying to imagine what he might be feeling as he takes his last meal and sleeps his final night.

The lobster lays "cruciform" on the table before going into the boiling water. Earlier, not knowing the French word for lobster, Belacqua uses "fish" when talking to the French teacher, noting, "Fish had been good enough for Jesus Christ, Son of God, Saviour. It was good enough for Mlle. Glain."[62] That alludes to the ancient *ichthys* symbol, a secret code for Jesus used by early Christians, which resembled a fish. Thus, the lobster is an icon of Christ crucified, Beckett's favorite symbol for the collective suffering of humanity and the injustices that plague existence.

"Dante and the Lobster" oozes with compassion for humanity as it reflects on the suffering and sorrows of life. It meditates on the stark disparity between God's justice and mercy with the symbol of Christ's crucifixion and McCabe's unjust execution. Reading this story in the light of Moltmann's theology offers an insightful perspective. Rather than indignation against God, the cruciform image of the lobster shows the presence of God even in the midst of the disparity, in the midst of suffering and death. How will God "solve" the problem of justice and mercy? That remains an open question, an open wound we all must bear. The point is not to solve it but to feel less forsaken, less lonely, in God-forsakenness. If we are a God-forsaken people, then God, in love, has become a God-forsaken God. If we are in hell, then Christ is too; as the Psalmist reflected, "If I bed down in Sheol—there You are" (Psalms 139:8).[63] That is the message of the cross, which Beckett reinforces beautifully. Belacqua did not know the lobster was alive, and we, too, are often unaware of Christ's solidarity with us even in the darkest hour of despair. It may not be a quick death, but it is also not a lonely one, nor is it without hope.

Offtish

Inspired by a sermon—or more accurately, repulsed by one—the poem *Offtish* (a play on the German "auf dem tisch," meaning, "on the table") invokes the call to offer up your suffering to the pot of collective human misery: "offer it up plank it down."[64] Beckett compiles a list of illnesses, trifles, and heart-aches, leading to a bitter conclusion, "it all boils down to the blood of the lamb." Harvey recounts the sermon that inspired the poem. A priest proclaimed: "What gets me down is pain. The only thing I can tell them is that the crucifixion was only the beginning. You must contribute to the kitty."[65]

The poem's vision is dark and blasphemous. Its agony and revolt against God for the endlessness of human misery is apparent. What sort of world is this? What sort of God demands so much pain from us? The poem is perhaps a prime example of Beckett's tendency to link suffering to Christ's cross. But, in a theological sense, we may read the final line differently from how Beckett intended. Rather than a rebuke against God, "it all boils down to the blood of the lamb" could be read according to the insight that God shares human suffering. Our misery is God's misery. The call to "offer it up" no longer has the cadence of hopelessness but of shared plight. If we imagine that our collective human suffering boils in a "pot," it is not wrong to call it the bitter "cup" of calvary, which Christ drank willingly. And what else would it be? On the night before Christ's crucifixion, He prayed, "My Father, if it is possible, let this cup pass from me; yet not what I want but what you want [...] My Father, if this cannot pass unless I drink it, your will be done" (Matt. 26:39, 42). All the horrors, agonies, cries, sufferings—each and every iota of human misery —such was Christ's cup for us, and such is the boundless depth of God's love. It is a cup of communion, not isolation. Indeed, if all human misery is in a pot, then it "boils down to the blood of the lamb"—the Lamb of God that takes away the sins of the world.

Breath

Beckett's texts frequently mourn the horror of inevitable death. It is a continual threat looming over human life. In Beckett's memorable phrase, "Birth was the death of him."[66] We may fill our time with meaningless activities and distractions to suppress our sense of finitude, but we cannot escape reality. We are all born "astride of a grave," and inevitably, "the light gleams an instant, then it's night once more."[67] Life unavoidably ends and often without warning: "No matter how no matter where. Time and grief and self so-called. Oh all to end."[68] Death is life's only certainty.

While much of Beckett's work stylistically mourns death, *Breath* is unique in that it successfully laments life's brevity without uttering a word. The play opens on a dimly lit stage littered with trash. A faint cry is heard, then a breath. Then another cry, echoing the first. An exhale. Then the light slowly goes out, and all is silence. Fade to black. The play is over in about thirty seconds. Death is a catastrophe and catharsis.

We far too often allow ourselves to slip into distraction, to fill our days with empty materialism or meaningless pursuits. We waste life when we fail to think of its end. "Nothing like breathing your last to put new life into you."[69] The remembrance of our limitations is essential in not losing our vigor for life. An unexamined life is not worth living, according to Socrates. Likewise, an unexamined death devalues life. Life is beautiful because it ends, our time is not unlimited, and we are bound to our humanity.

While Beckett sees life itself as a great sin, we can have a more generous appreciation of life. Even if life ends with death and there is nothing beyond, as even some theologians propose, it would not change the fact that God is with us in our finitude. Death may be an ever-present terror, but God is an unshakable foundation of hope. Our life may be as short as a single breath, but it is a life in which God waits for us in every moment. And because God is with us and waits for us, our life is eternally held in the remembrance of God. God does not forget us even in our finitude, even if we end in total oblivion. As Christian's we confess a simple hope: God is my beyond.

God is waiting for us in daily life. God embraces us as we are and not as we imagine we should be. We are human, finite, earthly beings, and God's grace is all the more astounding because God embraces us in our limitations. Moltmann writes, "I expect the presence of God in everything I meet and everything I do. His history with me, and with us, is an ongoing history."[70] That is our joy and hope, but if we distract ourselves and hide from our finitude, we cannot meet with God in the midst of life. An unobserved life and an unremembered death have the danger of leading us to reject God in the daily, mundane events of life. Life ends, but in the end—a new beginning.

Conclusion

By presenting a body of work focused on the poor, weak, destitute, and miserable, Samuel Beckett evokes empathy, compassion, and solidarity. The best approach to reading a writer like Beckett is not through the powers of intellectual astuteness, but with the weakness of human feeling. Accordingly, Beckett's artistic endeavor was to find a literary form for the mess of being. In an interview with Tom Driver, he explained, "To find a form that accommodates the mess, that is the task of the artists now."[71] Art is strong, a beautiful form, something acutely put. But reality is messy, weak, frail, and often grotesque. To combine the weak and strong, to put human misery in the heights of artistic creation—that was Beckett's aim. And behind this artistic endeavor, we find a keen sensitivity to suffering and despair.

This sensitivity is what makes reading Beckett such a moving experience. The director Alan Mandell once said to Beckett how glad he was to learn he was writing again after a long period of inactivity. But Beckett replied, "No, no, it's very painful, very difficult."[72] When pressed about why he finds writing such a struggle, Mandell remembers him saying, "Because it gets harder and harder to write a line that's honest."[73] Anthony Minghella likewise reflects on Beckett's fidelity to honesty, writing, "Everyone who loves Beckett will say the same thing: no matter how miserable or dark or cruel it appears, his work is also profoundly uplifting. It's honest, naked, leavened with mischief. And full of pity."[74] Beckett turns the status quo on its head. The height of his artistic achievement culminates in destitute, weak, honest words from a broken soul singing its song of lament.

In an astute observation, Martin Esslin remarked, "Sam had an absolutely mystical obligation towards that poor, suffering, enclosed being that doesn't know there is a way out."[75] There is indeed something profoundly spiritual in Beckett's quest to put the mess of being into an artistic form, to "write a line that's honest." It is rooted in an obligation to voice the sorrows of the poor and weak in our midst. When we read his work, we sense a deep vulnerability to human misery and compassion for suffering.

Theology has not taken seriously enough the problematic questions of suffering and grief. We do, of course, pay attention to it abstractly. We love to engage in speculative debates about the question of theodicy. But abstractions help no one, nor do they accurately reflect the real state of humanity. Cheap answers and reductionistic solutions to the problem of God and suffering have plagued the Church and disheartened many as a result.

For Moltmann, the only valid Christian response to the problem of suffering is to look to the cross, where God in Christ entered our God-forsaken spaces, became the brother of the damned and the friend of the forsaken. In Christ, we discover that suffering is not alien to God, as it was in the old theological notions of divine impassibility, but essential to the God who *is* love, the sort of love that dies on the cross. God is neither above us nor merely near us in our pain—God is with us and shares our sorrow.

Accordingly, Moltmann does not claim to have an answer for suffering. Only God can and will answer the theodicy question. But the real horror of suffering is not that it is intellectually unanswerable, but that we feel alone in our darkness. Moltmann calls this the "suffering in suffering," the bitter lack of love and sense of abandonment. He writes:

> For the suffering in suffering is the lack of love, and the wounds in wounds are the abandonment, and the powerlessness in pain is unbelief. And therefore the suffering of abandonment is overcome by the suffering of love, which is not afraid of what is sick and ugly, but accepts it and takes it to itself in order to heal it. Through his own abandonment by God, the crucified Christ brings God to those who are abandoned by God. Through his suffering he brings salvation to those who suffer. Through his death he brings eternal life to those who are dying. And therefore the tempted, rejected, suffering and dying Christ came to be the centre of the religion of the oppressed and the piety of the lost.[76]

The question of suffering and grief does not belong with the speculative philosophers. The problem of pain is not that we lack an overabundance of cheap answers attempting to explain away evil; rather, we lack solidarity. We feel alone and forsaken in our grief. But the realization that God suffers with us and takes our suffering into the inner life and love of the Trinity is a great comfort. As Bonhoeffer realized, "Only the suffering God can help."[77]

The distinction between solidarity and cheap answers is clear in Elie Wiesel's first-hand account of the holocaust, *Night*. Two men and a young boy were condemned to death by hanging in the camp. The two men died quickly, but the young boy suffered in agony for a long time. Wiesel recalls how it took about thirty minutes before he stopped breathing. The guards forced the prisoners to watch the horrible sight as it unfolded. He writes:

> Behind me, I heard the same man asking:
> 'For God's sake, where is God?'
> And from within me, I heard a voice answer:
> 'Where He is? This is where—hanging here from this gallows…'[78]

What else can we say in the face of such horrors? Abstractions are not only unhelpful in the light of this tragedy; they are deeply offensive. In response to this account, Moltmann writes:

> Any other answer would be blasphemy. There cannot be any other Christian answer to the question of this torment. To speak here of a God who could not suffer would make God a demon. To speak here of an absolute God would make God an annihilating nothingness. To speak here of an indifferent God would condemn men to indifference.[79]

In presenting one of the most profound expressions of human misery and suffering, Beckett has created a literary meditation both compassionate and empathetic, a testament of solidarity with those who suffer. Beckett does not offer a response from the "bargain basement" of philosophical explications. Instead, he places his hand over the wound and leaves no maggot lonely. The best sort of literature is not the kind that offers us an empty escape from brute reality but helps us feel less alone in our sorrow. That is Beckett's greatness as a writer. Solidarity in suffering is also a central point of comparison between his work and Jürgen Moltmann's theology. When we read of Didi and Gogo's loneliness and grief, we feel less alone in our own. The same is true when we read of Molloy's aimlessness, Pim's despair, Clov's confliction, and the lament of the unnamable voice crying alone in the dark. If we grow in our sensitivity to suffering and honesty about despair, we grow as human beings. There can be no higher moral goal for a writer than to evoke such empathy. Theologically, this inspires us to reflect more deeply on God's solidarity with us, the depth of God's co-suffering love. We cannot hide away from the brute realities of our world, nor should we be content with a cheap faith that accepts unquestioned answers.

The world is dark and difficult. Suffering and grief are unavoidable. To live is to suffer, to feel forsaken and alone in the darkness of this mess called existence. Yet, we are not alone. God has joined us in our darkness. God responds to human misery with solidarity, not cheap answers or excuses. But the Church and theology still have to learn that lesson. The Church is truly *Christ's* Church only in the company of the least of these. Our privileged flight from reality is a sinful denial of the bleeding heart of God in the poor and weak. As Vladimir reflected, "Was I sleeping, while the others suffered? Am I sleeping now?"[80] Let us not be caught sleeping. May we join the oppressed in their struggles. Their pain is God's pain. The rights of the poor are God's rights.

The world is dark, but God is in the darkness with us; our God is a God of the God-forsaken. And in this, we discover the most unquenchable hope of all, hope beyond hope, an unnamable hope. Beckett's work is bleak and full of suffering. It is not in spite of this fact that we should read him, but because of it. Yet readers frequently criticized his work for being too dark and depressing, too fixated on suffering. To this, Beckett responded:

> At a party an English intellectual—so-called—asked me why I write about distress. As if it were perverse to do so! He wanted to know if my father had beaten me or my mother had run away from home to give me an unhappy childhood. I told him no, that I had had a very happy childhood. Then he thought me more perverse than ever. I left the party as soon as possible and got into a taxi. On the glass partition between me and the driver were three signs: one asked for help for the blind, another, help for the orphans, and the third for relief for the war refugees. One does not have to look for distress. It is screaming at you even in the taxis of London.[81]

Beckett's literature is profoundly theological in its mystical attentiveness to the least of these. To turn a blind eye to suffering is to reject God, but to turn suffering into a speculative game is no less contemptible. Beckett's unrelenting visions of humanity on the brink of ruin and desolation shatters our frequent tendency to shy away from pain and distress. As such, he offers us one of the most beautiful lamentations since Ecclesiastes and the Psalms. Christ, too, waits for Godot.

2. SHE RAILS AT THE SOURCE OF ALL LIFE

PROTEST ATHEISM

Harold Pinter once explained to Beckett how his "writing seemed to him a constantly courageous attempt to impose order and form upon the wretched mess mankind had made of the world."[1] But Beckett denied having any such form. Instead, he replied, "If you insist on finding form, I'll describe it for you. I was in a hospital once. There was a man in another ward, dying of throat cancer. In the silence I could hear his screams continually. That's the only kind of form my work has."[2]

This hauntingly morbid yet perfectly apt image is a fitting summary of Beckett's writing. But lest we conclude it is too bleak, too nihilistic, to have anything to say theologically, we should recall that at the center of Christian faith, we find a far more haunting lament: "My God, my God, why have you forsaken me?" Like a man dying of cancer, crying out in protest against an indifferent, silent sky, Christ's lament is the prime example of what we will discuss in this chapter: protest atheism, or atheism for God's sake.

An anonymous victim of the Jewish Mauthausen concentration camp etched on its walls: "Wenn es einen Gott gibt muß er mich um Verzeihung bitten." Which means, "If there is a God, he will have to beg my forgiveness." It is not the philosopher's abstract questions that count in the face of tremendous tragedies. Instead, it is the cries in the dark, rebelling against the indifference of God and the injustices of existence. Theologically, we often pay more attention to the abstract questions of suffering and grief, but the bitter cries of protest from those who suffer should more forcefully occupy our attention. The philosopher asks, "Why do suffering and evil exist if God is good and powerful?" But the one who suffers cries, "Where is God?"

When we consider suffering abstractly, we default to cheap answers as if it were merely a problem to be solved. That manifests itself, in the theological sense, negatively and positively as cheap atheism and shallow fundamentalism. But these are two sides of the same coin. They are both desperate attempts to assert certainty in uncertainty. One says, "I know there is *no* God," while the other states, "I *know* there is a God." Yet both are founded on the same hubris. Each believes to have "proof" for God's existence or non-existence—having first assumed they can define what it means to be "God." In their hostility, what atheists and theists see in one another is their own folly reflected in a mirror. It is often the case that we are cut from the same cloth as our enemies. In the end, there is no substantial difference between dogmatic atheism and rigid fundamentalism.

But there is a third way. It must be possible to go beyond cheap certainties, embrace mystery open-heartedly, and reject dogmatism. There must exist a "beyond" where faith and doubt coexist as allies, not enemies. Beyond cheap atheism and empty theism, there is a theology of the cross and protest atheism. The false distinction between an atheist and theist is made obsolete by a depth of questioning that does not settle for cheap answers or shallow faith. It is here that Beckett and Moltmann share a fundamental conviction. Both thinkers refused to accept cheap answers to the open wound of human suffering. Instead, they plumb the depths of the bleeding heart of humanity and refuse to settle for easy ways out.

I aim to show here that Beckett is a protest atheist *par excellence.* His work expresses a protest against God that is not rightly identified with cheap atheism but with a kind of atheism for God's sake. Beckett was a God-haunted man, and the absence of God torments his work. As John Pilling writes, Beckett's atheism was not merely the denial of God but far more complex:

> Beckett's religious position is essentially a severe one. We have no way of telling exactly when his religious faith lapsed, but it is clear that from his earliest years he found death and suffering difficult to accommodate to

> the traditional idea of a benevolent God […] His response to what seemed a meaninglessly arbitrary, or worse, a derisory fiction [i.e., God], has taken many forms, but never […] a simple atheism. Just as he has been impressed by the faculty certain philosophers have for pursuing truth and facing the ultimate problems even after they have apparently been solved by system-building, so he has continued to be obsessed, personally, by the fundamentally religious questions concerning the existence of God, His justice and mercy, and the afterlife.[3]

Albert Camus rightly saw that the posture of metaphysical rebellion includes a "no" as well as a "yes." In other words, it is a no for the sake of a yes, an affirmation hidden in the midst of a negation. The rebel defies the absurdities of injustice, but in so doing, they also affirm that true justice is worthy of the struggle. The Biblical prophets share this impulse as they protested against God and the injustices of the world. Thus, the prophet and the protest atheist stand together against God in the name of God. This protest is a necessary aspect of the quest for truth and righteousness, without which we would settle for cheap substitutes. In the Hebraic tradition, protesting against God in the name of God is rooted in the refusal to turn God into an idol. Rejecting such a God is an act of holy resistance.

This protest in the name of God is an essential element of faith. Even protest *against* God in the name of justice affirms a God above God. That is what led Jürgen Moltmann to contemplate the notion of "protest atheism" in his classic work, *The Crucified God.* He admitted to feeling at home with this kind of atheism, helpfully comparing it to Job's wrestling with God.[4] In contrast with the shallow atheism of "banal consumerism"—like the trite "new atheists" of today who dogmatically reject God and mock those haunted by God's absence—there exists an atheism that protests against injustice *for God's sake.* While shallow atheists celebrate a world without God, protest atheists rebel against God-forsakenness and, in their rebellion, say "yes" to goodness and life in spite of absurdity. Moltmann writes:

> Crude atheism for which this world is everything is as superficial as the theism which claims to prove the existence of God from the reality of this world. Protest atheism points beyond both God and suffering,

> suffering and God, sets them one against the other and becomes an atheistic protest against injustice 'for God's sake'. In the context of the question which sets God and suffering over against each other, a God who sits enthroned in heaven in a glory that no one can share is unacceptable even for theology. [...] The only way past protest atheism is through a theology of the cross which understands God as the suffering God in the suffering of Christ and which cries out with the godforsaken God, 'My God, why have you forsaken me?'[5]

The philosopher Ernst Bloch considered himself an "atheist for God's sake." This confession, Moltmann recalls, "Took my breath away and later robbed me of my sleep, until I realized that a Jewish philosopher is bound to observe the Old Testament prohibition of images even in his thinking about God."[6] God is unnamable. In the Hebraic tradition, God is YHWH, that unspeakable symbol of God's otherness. That is the heart of protest atheism: it rebels against the idolatry of God in the name of God.

The Bible is full of cries of protest. From the Psalms to Job, the prophets, and especially Christ's cry from the cross, the Christian tradition is no stranger to protest atheism. As the Scriptures show time and time again, faith means struggle. Cheap faith is thus more dangerous to the Christian faith than atheism.

God cannot be domesticated. That idea is central not only for Hebraic theology but the dialectical theology of the twentieth century, of which Karl Barth and Paul Tillich were prominent figures. If God is unnamable and cannot become an object of human control, then God is always beyond our best thoughts about God. And that is what makes shallow atheism so untenable. It claims to name and reject God in the same breath. But such a rejection rests on a false premise about what it means to be God. The God whom atheists claim to deny is just as much an idol as the graven images rejected by the Scriptures. If God can be conceived in human terms and rejected accordingly, then such a God is no better than absolutized human ideals projected up into the heavens. Bonhoeffer warned about this when he wrote, "A god who could be proved by us would be an idol."[7] The reverse is also true: a God that could be disproved by human hands is an idol.

The true God remains beyond the provability or unprovability of human insight. We should be skeptical of anyone who claims either extreme, either the fundamentalists who claim to have proven God undeniably, or the atheists who have claimed to have disproven God beyond all doubt. Both are cut from the same bargain-basement cloth. Neither is acceptable for honest and sincere discussions of faith and theology. But protest atheism deserves a place in the Christian faith; it is closer to the theology of the cross than fundamentalism. As Bloch says, "Only an atheist can be a good Christian." To which Moltmann added, "Only a Christian can be a good atheist."[8] Indeed, protest atheism is a Christian obligation to stand against all false gods and human idols.

But this leads us to consider the question of Samuel Beckett's supposed atheism. Critics of his work often assume that there are only two alternatives; either Beckett is a traditional, orthodox Christian, or he is an atheist full stop. So while he is clearly not the former, he is often forced into the latter. Existentialist interpretations of his work abound and rely heavily on this faulty presupposition. But the problem remains what to do with the abundance of religious themes that overwhelm his texts. Some take far too seriously the excuse that these are merely a mythology Beckett used because it was one he was familiar with. This explanation ignores the outstanding depth of Beckett's engagement with these religious symbols. Beckett's work is profoundly spiritual *because of* its blasphemous rebellion against God's absence, not in spite of it.

So we must resist the temptation of limiting Beckett with a false either/or. As Sandra Wynands realized, "Denying God, or denying the God of the positive religions, does not in itself abolish transcendence."[9] Whatever kind of religiosity Beckett may claim or deny, the reality is his work exists beyond all cheap forms of theism or atheism. There is an unavoidably transcendent dimension to his writing. His characters are haunted by God in spite of God's supposed absence, as Richard Coe writes:

> The fact remains, however, that if Beckett is very far from being a Christian, he is equally far from being an atheist in any blunt materialistic sense. His people, without exception, are haunted and tortured by the idea of God.[10]

Jürgen Moltmann once argued that Christ's cry on the cross is either the *end* of theology altogether or the beginning of a genuinely *Christian* theology founded upon the suffering of the crucified God. Both Beckett and Moltmann exist beyond cheap atheism and empty theism. Beckett's God-haunted literature is just as iconoclastic. He throws down the gauntlet and draws a line between the shallows and depths. It is from this perspective that a theological appreciation of Beckett's protest becomes possible. Against God, for the sake of God, Beckett laments God's absence from the world. His work mirrors Christ's dying lament more than any other writer I know. If the Christian faith cannot empathize with Beckett's protest atheism, then it has no share in Christ's; the two are one.

My dear Sir, look—at the world—and look—at my trousers!

Beckett's novel *Watt,* composed in the south of France during the war, contains an early, pointed example of protest atheism. He wrote the book to keep sane amid so much insanity all around him. But it is a unique work in Beckett's canon, perhaps his funniest and most philosophical at once.

In the fourth chronological section of the book, Watt is in the garden with Sam, the narrator. Down by the stream, they make friends with rats. They give them food, and the rats begin to trust them and show signs of confidence and affection. So they begin to subject them to cannibalism, of which Sam concludes: "It was on these occasions, we agreed, after an exchange of views, *that we came nearest to God.*"[11]

It is a disturbing image even without Sam's final comment, but the comparison to God elevates the account to the level of metaphysical protest against the cruelties of creation. If God permits suffering and evil, and if God is still good and just, then God is either indifferent to suffering or willfully causes suffering. Some theologians with fatalistic tendencies will revel in the latter proposition, arguing that because something happens, it is God's will. And if it is God's will, then it is God's pleasure. Thus, God takes joy in horrors such as genocide, disease, and war. Indeed, such a God is no better than a demon.

A joke from *Endgame* offers another condemnation of the world and the God for whom it is to blame. Nagg begins, "An Englishman, needing a pair of striped trousers in a hurry for the New Year festivities, goes to his tailor who takes his measurements."[12] The tailor says to come back in four days, and it will be ready. After four days, he says to come back in another week, "I've made a mess of the seat." After a week, he says to come back in ten days, "I've made a hash of the crotch." After ten days, the pants are still not ready, and he says to come back in a fortnight, "I've made a balls of the fly." Finally, the Englishman explodes at the tailor:

> 'God damn you to hell, Sir, no, it's indecent, there are limits! In six days, do you hear me, six days, God made the world. Yes Sir, no less Sir, the world! And you are not bloody well capable of making me a pair of trousers in three months!' To this the tailor replies, 'But my dear Sir, my dear Sir, look—at the world—and look—at my trousers!'[13]

The implication is that the world was a botched job and full of mistakes, while the trousers, which took longer, are a superior creation. Much of Beckett's protest atheism revolves around this idea that the world's woes are reason enough to blame God for its failure. Behind this lies the well-known conclusion that if the world is full of suffering and God does nothing, God is either incapable of helping or unwilling to. In either case, the world is a mistake, and God is no better than Watt feeding young rats to their parents. However, Beckett's texts are not resigned to accepting this absurdity without protest, as Beckett explained to an actor about *Endgame*, "Hamm says No! against the nothingness."[14] Beckett's work is never without this No. He may place front and center the woes and miseries of human existence, but he protests against the darkness rather than accepting it with nihilistic resignation.

These examples are similar to the metaphysical rebellion of Dostoyevsky's Ivan, which was, for Moltmann, the classic example of protest atheism in literature.[15] Ivan returned his ticket and refused to accept a world full of suffering. "It's not God that I don't accept, Alyosha, only I most respectfully return him the ticket." The impossibility of harmonizing an unjust world with a God of justice and love is the bedrock of protest atheism, its constant cry and unanswered plea. What Ivan rejects is not the idea of God in itself but the absurdity of reconciling such a God with such a world. Beckett's protest atheism is the same. As one critic recognized in *Endgame,* "More than anything else, it seemed to me to be, in a sense, a kind of tragic poem, man's last prayer to a God that might or might not exist."[16] The refusal to reconcile himself with either the cruelty of this world or the absurd absence of God is at the heart of Beckett's protest atheism.

How It Is

A voice murmurs in the mud; a body crawls, pants, is tormented, and torments others under a silent sky with images of life above in the light, taunting life below in the stark reality of a dark, destitute world. That is the world of *How It Is.* The book is one of Beckett's most original, especially in his clever use of phrasing and pace. The text is entirely unpunctuated to evoke a sense of breathless panting, the mud-murmurings of a desperate soul. It is a brutal and beautiful work, which Harold Bloom considered among Beckett's best. But it is also one of Beckett's most sustained indictments against God and the world. As Laura Barge writes, "In *How It Is* Beckett implicates God as being ultimately responsible for each facet of this consummate failure more clearly than in any other fictional work."[17] The world of *How It Is* is God-forsaken and cruel, yet it is also supremely God-haunted and longs for a God who never manifests. The one responsible for such a world is no God at all but a demon. *How It Is* fictionalizes what the world would be like if Satan created it, and in forcing the comparison to our world, it becomes one of Beckett's most brutal protests against God. As John Pilling explains:

> God, if he exists, must clearly be omnipotent and omniscient. In the world of *How it is* he is the one who (hypothetically) provides the sacks. But *How it is* is a savage parody of the Leibnizian idea that this is the best of all possible worlds, a panorama of aggressor and victim perpetually encircling a world based on cruelty. It is more like the worst of all possible worlds [...] Beckett stresses that only one half of the divine contract is fulfilled: He is just ('that's our justice,' says the voice of *How it is* with outraged regularity), but not merciful. [...] God, in conceiving the world, brought forth suffering, and it would be better for us all not to have been born. Beckett's attitude, is gnostic or manichean. The God who created the world was Satan.[18]

Treading aimlessly about in the mud, crawling from one muck heap to another, that is the miserable plight of Beckett's characters. But is our world any different? That is likely the question Beckett wanted us to consider when reading the text. In a parody of Leibniz's "best of all worlds," Beckett seems to imply that this is not the best—nor even an acceptable world; this is the worst of all worlds. If we remove the facades, it is hard to argue that our earth is better than the bleak reality of *How It Is*. The scenery may change, but it's always the same muck. As Molloy reflected, "But it's a change of muck. And if all muck is the same muck that doesn't matter, it's good to have a change of muck[.]"[19] We belong to the muck heap—of mud we are, and to mud we must return. Or, in the words of Scripture, "For you are dust, and to dust shall you return" (Genesis 3:19).[20] In a sense, then, *How It Is* is a creative re-telling of Genesis, but instead of establishing God's goodness and glory, it protests against the world God made. In Beckett's account, creation is not the proof of God's greatness but God's sin, the sin of birth. There may be traces of a "light" above, a false hope, but we are stuck in the primordial mud of the earth. As Hamm declared, "You're on earth, there's no cure for that!"[21] Such is the bitter lament of *How It Is.*

A subtle God-consciousness haunts the narrator's thoughts nonetheless. The fourth paragraph describes an "ancient voice in me not mine[.]"[22] His is "a life" "given" by another.[23] The narrator separates life in the mud from "the other above in the light said to have been mine[.]"[24] Images from that other life come to him in the dark. But even that is questionable because these are not memories, "I haven't been given memories this time," but rather poetic images, "it was an image the kind I see sometimes see in the mud[.]"[25] That establishes a powerful myth-making tendency to the story. It also subverts the narrative to such a degree that Barge concluded, "*How It Is* is a novel primarily about the art of language."[26] The narrator seems conscious of being a fictional identity listening to stories spoken by a voice in the dark. But he is bound to the muck to be haunted by these false images. That life spoken to him in the mud is itself a form of torment, a kind of Dantesque hell. The narrator's God-consciousness persists throughout the novel, but God is starkly absent, even if the consciousness of God remains. God's breath infused the world with life, but with that same God-breathed breath, the narrator curses life in the mud and protests being born.

The narrator tries to comfort himself by recalling the way his mother used to quote Scripture, "upcast to the sky whence cometh our help and which I know perhaps even then with time shall pass away[.]"[27] And he tries to pray as she taught him, "in a word bolt upright on a cushion on my knees whelmed in a nightshirt I pray according to her instructions[.]"[28] This image is autobiographical. Beckett's mother once had him sit in a praying position so she could take a picture of her pious son.[29] But Beckett never could live up to the piety of his harsh mother. The narrator also wrestles with a faith forced upon him, his mother's prayers in his mouth, yet it is an empty gesture devoid of any sense of comfort it once evoked.

There is a parting reference to the myth of Erebus and the philosopher Heraclitus the Obscure that further implicates God in the God-forsaken misery of the world. Erebus was the God of darkness and shadow. If the world is the product of a God, then it is the God of darkness, and thus a God that is no better than a demon. And those in the mud are left to weep and wail their miseries to a silent sky, like Heraclitus the Obscure, often called the "weeping philosopher." Both allusions highlight the general mood of a world abandoned by God and of a people left alone to weep in the darkness, wailing against their creator.

The narrator tries to pray again, but without success, which leads him to think of the damned:

> prayer in vain to sleep I have no right to it yet I haven't deserved it prayer for prayer's sake when all fails when I think of the souls in torment true torment true souls who have no right to it no right ever to sleep we're talking of sleep I prayed for them once if I may believe an old view it has faded[30]

For most of Beckett's characters, death is both a relief that never comes and an inevitable terror. If life itself under a God-forsaken sky is damned, and the only sin is the sin of being born, then death is release and freedom. Death is the great terror and relief of life, catastrophe and catharsis. Beckett's literature curses God for making such a miserable world, as the narrator implicitly does throughout the text. Yet he never finds release and seems instead to be condemned to go on alone in the dark without hope of death's healing. A fleeting reference to Abraham's bosom a page later hints towards a familiar fear of Beckett's characters, the fear that life goes on even after death, that release never truly comes.

The work culminates in the first of several direct indictments against God, "curse God no sound make mental note of the hour and wait midday midnight curse God or bless him and wait watch in hand[.]"[31] Jesus makes an appearance as well from some kind of dream, "wake up in a sweat and have met Jesus in a dream[.]"[32] Before the close of the first section "before Pim," another curse bursts forth, "curse God bless him beseech him no sound[.]"[33] This lament seems to hold out two conflicting possibilities. First is the instinct to curse God for existence, then the old religious guilt comes back imploring the narrator to bless God and beseech mercy, but the kicker comes with the simple but devastating realization: "no sound[.]" God is silent, and that is the epitome of God's sin. Two sections later, the narrator looks for a "celestial tin miraculous sardines sent down by God at the news of my mishap wherewith to spew him out another week[.]"[34] God is longed for yet also cursed for being absent. A consciousness for God remains, but no God to fill the void. However, this protest against God is at once a striving after a God beyond God. There is a God-shaped absence looming over all of Beckett's work, and here it is felt with unique potency.

In part two, we learn the narrator's name, or at least what Pim is allowed to call him, "Bom he can call me Bom[.]"[35] Several pages later, an image of "tender years" arises that speaks of early faith:

> a moment of the tender years the lamb black with the world's sins the world cleansed the three persons yes I assure you and that belief the feeling since then ten eleven that belief said to have been mine the feeling since then vast stretch of time that I'd find it again the blue cloak the pigeon the miracles he understood [...] the childhood the belief the blue the miracles all lost never was[36]

The "vast stretch of time" motif is an agent of hopelessness, loss, and decay. Time, or more precisely habit, is the great deadener, as Beckett noted in his Proust essay. Whatever belief was once held, in either Bom or Beckett himself (we sense a bit of autobiography here), has been "all lost never was" to the sands of time (or perhaps we should say to the mud of time). *How It Is* laments time's tendency to destroy faith and turn hope for God into a bitter rebellion against God's absence. It evokes a perpetual dark night of faith, in which Beckett's entire literary canon lives.

A curious section seems to allude to the crucifixion, though it may be a stretch. We read, "God on God desperation utter confusion did he believe he believed then no couldn't any more his reasons both cases my God[.]"[37] Christ's lament from the cross, his utter confusion, and desperation before God's absence may be said to be a kind of God against God ("God on God"). That is a possible reading of these lines. Even the final phrase "my God" seems to evoke the death cry of Christ's crucifixion, as well as the sense of doubt and confusion that preceded it. Indeed, that same desperation is echoed in Bom's despair over this God-forsaken world. Two paragraphs down, we read another haunting question, "God in heaven yes or no if he loved me a little if Pim loved me a little yes or no[.]"[38] Bom asks if God is in heaven, then seems to ask either if God loves him or if Pim loves him. Either reading carries an emotional effect. The yearning to be loved with the lack of any such certainty points to Bom's protest against the absurdity of existence. There remains a longing for certainty, like the longing for God, but no means of satisfaction. Neither a yes nor no is spoken. Assurance is never known. Yet we go on in the mud crawling into the unknown as these vast stretches of time wear us down to nothing. It is either the end of God or the discovery of a God beyond God.

We again hear from Bom's religious mother, "mama none either column of jade bible invisible in the black hand only the edge red gilt the black fingers inside psalm one hundred and something oh God man his days as grass flower of the field wind above in the clouds[.]"[39] That is a reference to Psalms 103:15, "As for mortals, their days are like grass; they flourish like a flower of the field; for the wind passes over it, and it is gone, and its place knows it no more. But the steadfast love of the Lord is from everlasting to everlasting on those who fear him." Later, Bom refers to Ecclesiastes, arguably the book of the Bible that has the most in common with Beckett's work, "I remembered my days an handbreath my life as nothing man a vapour[.]"[40] In Scripture: "All is mere breath."[41]

As part two comes to a close, a familiar theme arises, namely, the inability to go on yet the necessity to: "one can't go on one goes on as before can one ever stop put a stop that's more like it one can't go on one can't stop put a stop[.]"[42] Pim is soon departing, and Bom will again be alone in the dark: "nothing left but words a murmur on and off[.]"[43] Bom interrogates Pim:

> if he talks to himself no if he thinks no believes in God yes every day no wishes to die yes but doesn't expect to no he expects to stay where he is yes flat as a cow clap on his belly yes in the mud yes without motion yes without thought yes eternally yes […] if he wants to leave him yes[44]

True paralysis is achieved, and Pim remains alone in the mud motionless for all eternity. Or so he hopes.

Part three, "after Pim," is full of crosses and tormentors: "several lives crosses everywhere indelible traces[.]"[45] The tormentors seem to take over the narrative, "vast stretch of time nothing stirring save the tormentors[.]"[46] But each person is both oppressor and victim. Bom himself engages in tormenting and is tormented, just as each person in the mud continues the cycle. The world is not only tortured by its lack of God, but it is full of violent people. *How It Is* meditates on suffering and absurdity from every angle. God is absent, suffering is unavoidable, companionship is doomed, and people are reduced to objects.

How It Is is an extreme example of protest against God and life, arguably more devastating than Dostoevsky's Ivan. Even the self is in question, as Bom reflects on the possibility that he is nothing but a voice, a murmur spoken in the dark, "I hear me again murmur me in the mud and am again[.]"[47] We are not even at home in ourselves in this world. Our loneliness is boundless; our alienation stark. We are objects unto ourselves. Are we nothing more than the stories we tell ourselves in the dark? The story of our life in the light as we progress through time? Are we all more like Bom crawling in the mud than we think? These seem to be the questions Beckett raises with this text. Neither God nor neighbor nor world nor self are free from the cruelty of suffering under a silent, God-forsaken sky. We frequently avoid meditating on these questions, but Beckett's protest forces us to consider the bleak realities of life in an unjust, uncertain world. By lifting the ideological veil, he reveals the dark underbelly of reality. But the truth can also set us free, as Christ taught. It is better to have our noses rubbed in the mud and muck of existence than bury our heads in it, dreaming of another world.

An "ancient voice ill-spoken ill-heard murmur ill" is heard again as the end becomes inevitable.[48] Bom even contemplates and hopes for "a love" from "one not one of us an intelligence somewhere[,]" a divine being of sorts "who all along the track at the right places according as we need them deposits our sacks[.]"[49] But this cry seems to go unanswered. The end is unavoidable: "inconceivable end of this immeasurable wallow[.]"[50] In the text's final pages, the narrator seems to realize that he is nothing but a fiction told in the dark. He is not even Bom, and cries out, "WHAT'S MY NAME[?]"[51] Nonetheless, he moves onward towards his end. In a final act of total deconstruction, we read:

> only me in any case yes alone yes in the mud yes the dark yes that holds yes the mud and the dark hold yes nothing to regret there no with my sack no I beg your pardon no no sack either no not even a sack with me no[52]

The narrator is alone. Panting in the dark in the progression of "worse and worse[,]" his arms are spread "like a cross[.]"[53] This final cruciform image is a potent summary of the entire text. The cross is an image of God-forsakenness and the death of God. It is also the beginning point for discovering a God beyond God, the God beyond the protest of God. God in Christ joins us in our laments and protests against an absent God and instead proclaims God's solidarity with humanity in our suffering. God is not in heaven but down in the mud with Bom and all of us. God is the victim in the muck tormented by the tormentors. Christ, too, protests against the indifferent, impassible God.

The cross is a key image, if not *the* key image, in *How It Is.* That is clear not only from the themes of suffering, God-abandonment, and cries of despair but in the cruciform images that we find throughout the text. For example, the sardines in the sack evoke the early Christian symbol of a fish for Christ and act as a kind of manna from heaven. Even the act of crawling in the mud is an image of a helpless figure in a semi-cruciform shape. There is also an explicit reference to St. Andrew's cross in the text, the Scottish cross shaped like an X rather than a lower-case T. When someone crawls on their belly through the mud, they inevitably form the same shape. Thus, the entire book is about a cruciform figure struggling under a God-forsaken sky, tormented, abandoned, and haunted by the absence of God. *How It Is* is at once a profound work of protest against the silence of God and, if read theologically, an affirmation of Christ's solidarity with us in the muck of suffering. God is not in heaven above, in the light, distant from our pain. God takes up our cause in Jesus Christ and joins us in the mud. Christ is the sustenance (the sardines) and the means (the cross) of our struggle, yet it is precisely for this reason that there is a hope beyond hope, beyond the cheap hopes we give ourselves: hope for resurrection on the other side of the darkness of a God-forsaken death.

Catastrophe

The voice of *Not I* erupts in laughter at the idea of a "merciful God." *Rockaby* mourns life and pleads escape with its refrain, "rock her off," concluding with a forceful rejection of life, "Fuck life." *Breath* dramatizes the brevity of life in a thirty-second icon of chaos. *A Piece of Monologue* contemplates the tragedy of birth, "Birth was the death of him." The short piece, *Lessness,* ends with a figure facing down the empty void, cursing God, "face to endlessness [...] He will curse God again as in the blessed days."[54] Beckett's work abounds with examples of protest and rebellion against the state of the world and the God who abandoned it.

Catastrophe is a particularly apt example of protest atheism. Beckett dedicated this play to Václav Havel, a politician and playwright imprisoned for his struggle against totalitarianism. Even though political protest is the most apparent interpretation of the play, we can also read it as an example of metaphysical rebellion. The word "catastrophe" often implies simply a "disaster," but that is not Beckett's intended meaning. Instead, it reflects the old use of the word, which originates from Aristotle. Here, a catastrophe is an action evoking ruin and pain on stage. It is thus not merely a tragic event but more like a sadistic endurance test. Malone reflected on a "veritable catastrophe that has befallen me." He has lost his stick. And explains, "Catastrophe too in the ancient sense no doubt. To be buried in lava and not turn a hair, it is then a man shows what stuff he is made of."[55] This concept of catastrophe is thus connected with the act of protest. To show what one is made of in the face of absurdity means standing up in defiance against the cosmic tormentor.

Catastrophe shows the dehumanization of a man called "P" by a director and his assistant. They treat P as an object, alienated from self and society to be observed and controlled. Even his name is depersonalized. The director and assistant prepare him to stand before a crowd, and after an absurd series of alterations in his appearance and stance, he is deemed ready for the performance. But at the moment of his reveal, P rebels against his captors. He raises his head ever so slightly in the final moments of the play, staring down his public with a glare of fiery rebellion. His stare silences the cheering crowd. By raising his head, he acts in a small but profound gesture of resistance and free will to show he is a man and not a thing. Thus, the director and his assistant's extreme physical and psychological control over P is broken with a defiant act.

Beckett himself described P's final movement not as an appeal for release, as some assumed, but as an act of protest: "He is a triumphant martyr rather than a sacrificial victim [...] and is meant to cow onlookers into submission through the intensity of his gaze and stoicism."[56] P's glare of resistance is like the victorious martyr who has won out against his oppressor by refusing to accept their terms, even to the point of death. That is like the rebellion of a protest atheist. Unable to reconcile God and a corrupt world, the protest atheist refuses to accept things as they are. They paradoxically accept their unacceptable condition because they must live in this world, but they do not consent to it. The protest atheist says No to nothingness. They protest despite being unable to; they go on when they cannot go on, saying yes to existence despite its absurdity.

Ill Seen Ill Said

A final example comes from what is arguably Beckett's late masterpiece, *Ill Seen Ill Said.* This minimalist prose poem tells of a mythological, almost saintly woman who bears the suffering of human history and mourns the fleeting mortality of existence. Beckett introduces the theme of protest in the first paragraph: "She rails at the source of all life."[57]

But the text is less of a story than it is an image, or better still, a kind of religious icon. We catch fleeting glimpses and impressions of events, which gives the work a profoundly poetic tendency. *It is* poetry, actually, or more aptly, prose poetry. Knowlson writes, "This meticulously woven tapestry of words is best read as an exquisite prose poem."[58] The French literary tradition is more familiar with prose poetry, and so the work can seem somewhat foreign to Anglophone ears. But it is crucial to think of it not as a novel but as a poem. Study the first few lines, and you can see why:

> From where she lies she sees Venus rise. On. From where she lies when the skies are clear she sees Venus rise followed by the sun. Then she rails at the source of all life. On. At evening when the skies are clear she savors its star's revenge.[59]

When read aloud, the poetry is evident. But if we put it into verse and note the accents, it is even more apparent:

From whére she líes
she sêes Vénus ríse.
Ón.
From whére she líes
when the skíes are cléar
she sêes Vénus ríse
fóllowed by the sún.
Then she ráils at the sóurce of âll life.
On.
At évening when the skíes are cléar
she sávors its stár's revénge.[60]

This opening paragraph alone contains six dimeter lines (five of which rhyme) and three trimeter lines primarily made up of anapests, which are bound together by alliterating spirants: "she lies," "she sees Venus rise" (twice), "skies" (twice), "sun," "she rails," "source," "she savors," "stars." The refrain word *on* punctuates the verse and also rhymes with "sun." Thus, Ruby Cohn is justified in calling *Ill Seen Ill Said* "The Beckett Masterwork."[61] It is certainly among his best.

As a poem, the text is less literal and more symbolic or iconic. Thus, Beckett's early interest in filmmaking shines through. (As a young man, he wrote the great Russian director Sergei Eisenstein, offering to work with him.) That is why, when considering the incredible number of religious images the work evokes, it is no stretch to call it a kind of iconographic poem of human misery and protest. In other words, it is a God-haunted image, a religious icon where, unlike traditional icons, God is most glaringly present in God's absence. Thus, the text mourns the death of God and protests the absurd misery of human suffering.

Beckett describes the woman of the poem as if she were a divine figure, with an iconic "halo of hair." Yet she is homely and domestic, too. Thus, she is like Mary, the mother of God. Notably, she evokes the image of a mobile Pietà, of Mary grieving the death of Christ. In the text, the woman, dressed in black, lays flowers on a gravesite. Her movements are slow and meditative, like that of a desert mystic or a mourning widow. At one point, a white lamb begins to follow her, "Reared for slaughter,"[62] and twelve figures, called "guardians," encircle her continually like the dials on a clock. These symbols recall Christ, the Lamb of God, and His twelve disciples, themselves a reference to the twelve tribes of Israel. The clock symbol seems to hint towards time's end, an eschatological motif. A growing number of white rocks also surround her cabin, recalling the Rock of Salvation, another image of Christ. But these are also tombstones, which means they are another eschatological reference. The long black coat the woman wears is a man's coat, most likely belonging to whoever lies in the grave. That may evoke Paul's famous imperative to "put on Christ" (Romans 13:14). It also indicates how she bears the weight of human suffering with each meditative step.

The woman's cabin is small, and she frequently gazes out the window towards the stars. Central to the cabin is a fish-shaped hook where she sometimes rests her coat. Beckett explicitly links the hook to the crucifixion: "All set to serve again. Like unto its glorious ancestors. At the place of the Skull. One April afternoon."[63] Beckett repeatedly describes it as being "nailed" to the mantle: "pisciform it hangs by its hook from a nail."[64] It is central to the cabin and thus to the meditation of Beckett's text. It represents the suffering of humanity, as Christ and the cross frequently represented for Beckett.

Beckett combines the theme of suffering and grief with overtones of eschatology, the end of the world, a standard comparison in his texts. The story evokes a sense of being, "Well on the way to inexistence."[65] John Banville recognized the work as "an extended poetic meditation on eschatology."[66] It evokes an image of humanity coming to an end in this particular woman's end, as she grieves loss yet embraces with joy the unavoidable. She is happy and triumphant when it all comes to an apocalyptic conclusion:

> Farewell to farewell. [...] First last moment. Grant only enough remain to devour all. Moment by glutton moment. Sky earth the whole kit and

> boddle. Not another crumb of carrion left. Lick chops and basta. No. One moment more. One last. Grace to breathe that void. Know happiness.[67]

Ill Seen Ill Said is not merely Beckett's most remarkable literary masterpiece; it is a *spiritual* masterpiece. The images evoked are profound and moving, and it is impossible to ignore the haunting sense of God's absence. Yet absence is not pure negation. It may be a dark icon of divine abandonment, as Sandra Wynands argued,[68] but it is an icon nonetheless. Thus, it would not be inaccurate to call this the height of Beckett's spiritual literature. Few works present such a moving testament to the modern longing for God amid the absence of God.

The text "rails at the source of all life" with its meditative obsession with suffering and grief. But it is a subtler indictment against God than those previously discussed. Unlike the bitter protest of *How It Is,* here Beckett mourns the unacceptable state of the world rather than merely rejecting it. It is a more delicate, but no less severe, protest against God. The woman mourns life's finitude as a surrogate for all humanity. Thus, in a sense, she lays flowers not on any individual's grave but on *the* grave we all share. Humanity may erect monuments and tombstones for persons, but the earth is our collective grave, from dust to dust. We walk, day in and day out, on our very tomb. But there is a sense of yearning conveyed by this truth as well. The text not only mourns death's inevitability; it longs for it. In a moving passage, we read:

> Let her vanish. And the rest. For good. And the sun. Last rays. And the moon. And Venus. Nothing left but black sky. White earth. Or inversely. No more sky or earth. Finished high and low. Nothing but black and white. Everywhere no matter where. But black. Void. Nothing else. Contemplate that. Not another world. Home at last. Gently gently.[69]

Home at last. Herein we discover the desire for unspeakable home, rooted in disdain for this suffering and diseased existence. The continual contemplation of death and the imminent void of nonbeing reflects Beckett's common refrain that life itself is lamentable because it is so short, yet death is embraced as a relief. As the narrator in Beckett's *Texts for Nothing* lamented, "I won't hear, I won't understand, all dies so fast, no sooner born."[70] Or movingly, in *Malone Dies,* the narrator recalls when he learned the names of the days as a child: "when they taught me the names of the days and I marveled at their being so few and flourished my little fists, crying out for more, and how to tell the time, and what are two or three days, more or less, in the long run, a joke."[71] This lament is familiar in Beckett's texts, but it pervades like a fog over *Ill Seen Ill Said.*

Beckett's world is God-haunted, but the absence of God is a weight of more profound heaviness than any presence. As Barge writes, "God may not exist, but we cannot escape the conclusion that Beckett's void that houses the ultimate reality is God-shaped, and thus could be filled only by a God."[72] Beckett's texts paradoxically affirm the nearness of God by evoking the weight of God's absence. For Beckett, the greatest sin God ever committed was not existing, and he continually holds it against Him. The poem beautifully captures that lament.

Conclusion

"It is only the desire, the passion, the thirst for God," according to Moltmann, "which turns suffering into conscious pain and turns the consciousness of pain into a protest against suffering."[73] There is a deep passion for God behind Beckett's concern for suffering and his protest against it. That is also what Helmut Thielicke recognized about Beckett, noting how, in *Waiting for Godot,* "the God question is the true if hidden theme."[74] As Thielicke later concludes, though not directly in regards to Beckett, "God is fundamentally the answer to the question enclosed in human existence. He is not identical with the answer man himself gives, no matter how pious or religious."[75] Beckett understood that no answer we give to ourselves could fill the void. Neither shallow atheism nor cheap faith adequately corresponds to the depth of questioning and suffering that lies in the heart of humanity. While he did not go so far as recognizing God as the goal of his pursuit, his work is profoundly spiritual in its protest of every human-made God that tries to fill that space. The absence of God haunts Beckett's world; God is the omni-absent one, the silent sky, the empty no-thingness. But if God is the answer we cannot give ourselves, then this state of perpetual iconoclasm against all human-made gods is a deeply theological impulse. The denial of all cheap answers makes way for the arrival of that which only God can give.

John Pilling aptly called Beckett a "God-haunted man," and thus, he unknowingly compared him to another great God-haunted man, St. Augustine.[76] In one of his most profound reflections on faith, Augustine imagines God saying to him, "Take heart; you would not be seeking Me if I had not already found You." I would cautiously argue that the same is true of Beckett, or at the very least of the characters in his work. In this light, Beckett's protest against God is a deeply religious and theological act, a kind of literary atheism for God's sake. Behind the mocking jokes, grotesque condemnations, and obscene comparisons lies a God-haunted center. For all his irreverence, Beckett mourns the loss of God more profoundly than most so-called spiritual writers. That does not make Beckett a believer—such a conclusion would be negligent and naive. But as I stated earlier, that is not the only alternative to cheap atheism. The religious spectrum is much richer than the dogmatic fundamentalists assume. In the shallows, there are only two positions, absolutely denying or affirming God's existence. But when we plunge into the depths, the picture is far more difficult to untangle. Yet it is also far more beautiful. We could ignore the plethora of Christian symbols and religious allusions in Beckett's work, but that would mean resigning Beckett to the shallows of interpretation and thus robbing his work of its spiritual beauty.

Like Augustine, Beckett would have no protest against God if he did not also have some sense for God—however blasphemous it may be. But blasphemy against a false God can be a kind of religious obligation, a holy duty. His sense-for-God does not take on a traditional form by any means, but his work involves the pursuit of the "God above God," the God not made by human hands, *the Unnamable.*

A theological appreciation of Samuel Beckett must come to terms with his protest against the idolatry of God. Such a God is indeed contemptible. But we should also recognize a hidden longing for God amid such a fierce rebellion against God. It is a protest for God's sake, whether Beckett realized it or not. Modern theology, too, has protested against this God. Jürgen Moltmann has called any such God of indifference a "demon" because this God remains silent in the face of human suffering. In this sense, Beckett is an ally to modern theology and its pursuit of a non-objectifiable God. We can no longer be content with the old definitions of God as indifferent and impassible. The indifference of God was shattered by the "passion of the passionate Christ." God is not apathetic to human misery but suffers under it and takes it into the very heart of God. As Moltmann writes, "There is no suffering which in this history of God is not God's suffering; no death which has not been God's death in the history on Golgotha."[77] All of human history has been taken up into the history of God; all suffering and death have become God's through the cross of Christ.

Thus, God is not like Watt and Sam as they delight in cannibalizing rats; God is, instead, like the rats slaughtered and fed. This grotesque image cannot escape its blasphemous comparison with Holy Eucharist—and perhaps it is closer to what the Lord's Supper should evoke. The Church has often sterilized the scandal of Christ's hard words, which turned away thousands, "Very truly, I tell you, unless you eat the flesh of the Son of Man and drink his blood, you have no life in you" (John 6:53). Indeed, Christ did not suffer and die between two candles on a pristinely maintained altar.[78] He bore a bloody and brutal end. And with His last, He cried out in protest, "Why have you forsaken me?" Beckett's protest atheism is not unlike Christ's cry of God-abandonment. In many respects, if we cannot appreciate Beckett's defiant iconoclasm, then we likely do not have a place for Christ's either.

3. UNSPEAKABLE HOME

QUEST AND DECONSTRUCTION

Beckett's subtle spirituality is more profound than his critics have assumed. It is not true that he only superficially borrows religious mythology for his writing; there is an unmistakable depth to his engagement with the questions of faith and theology. As Sandra Wynands realized, the notion that faith must necessarily be at odds with Beckett's work is false. Indeed, as we are beginning to see, Beckett's writing is profoundly spiritual, and his quest for truth reaches mystical heights often unmatched by other seekers after the truth. Thus, there not only can be but must be a sense of spiritual appreciation for Beckett and his work. Perhaps, we may even learn something from his relentless iconoclasm. Wynands explains:

> Adherents of traditional spiritual traditions have much to learn from the rigor with which Beckett approaches art as spiritual practice. In the end it is up to each reader to affirm God through his or her own act of faith and, surprisingly, to find no contradiction at all with what Beckett affirms differently in his work.[1]

Beckett's strange spirituality is most clearly on display with the persistent motif of the quest. The imperative his characters live under is the command to go on, despite being unable to. Whatever the object of their quest—whether it is an abstraction like the self or oblivion or a concrete reality like one's mother or Molloy—the unending constant is the imperative to go on. Even if there is no apparent goal to the quest, as in *How It Is,* the quest-imperative remains. It is a given in Beckett's literary world that we go on despite being unable to.

This motif is unmistakably spiritual. It shares its impulse with two important Christian traditions: negative (apophatic) theology and mysticism. We know from Beckett's library and reading habits that mysticism was a life-long interest, and Mary Bryden has shown the influence of mystics such as Thomas á Kempis, Julian of Norwich, St. John of the Cross, and the anonymous author of *The Cloud of Unknowing* on Beckett's work. Baldwin has likewise highlighted his considerable usage of mystical expressions. But more fundamentally, for all Beckett's characters, there is the shared sense of the ineffable. It is an invisible thread that ties them together. They share a hunger for the unknown and unknowable, which remains ever unsatisfied with cheap substitutes. They strive to name the unnamable or speak the ineffable. This drive also rests at the heart of negative theology and Christian mysticism. Beckett's artistic pursuit for the literature of failure or the "unword" is essentially a mystical quest for what lies beyond sense and nonsense, which, by definition, can exist only in the realm of the spiritual.

Wynands shows how Beckett's approach shares much with negative theology: "Beckett's texts bear the same mark of irreducibility as does the divine in the texts of negative theology."[2] God's transcendent irreducibility is foundational to the theological method of *via negativa,* the negative way of theological inquiry. Negative theology seeks to know God not by saying what God is but according to what God is not. St. Hilary of Poitiers helps us see the reasons for this method: "Finite minds cannot conceive of the Infinite." And elsewhere: "[T]he best combination of words we can devise cannot indicate the reality and the greatness of God."[3] Thus, negative theology is often called "apophatic" theology, which means "to deny to speak." Because God is quantitatively distinct from humankind, to speak of God is to fail to speak of God because our finite mind cannot conceive the infinite. Only by negation can finite minds *begin* to grasp the contours of divinity. God is beyond our greatest thoughts of God. As Wynands goes on to explain:

> For negative theology, what is at stake in this process is to safeguard God's transcendence: to keep him in a realm that is not of the order of

> beings (even if that be the order of a *supreme* being) and thus to emphasize that God will neither fit into nor answer to the patterns of human conceptuality. Thus Beckett and negative theology both understand that there cannot be a question of the *existence* of God (or of his nonexistence, for that matter), for the term 'existence' implies the order of *existents,* of beings.[4]

Modern theologians such as Paul Tillich have taken this to heart. Tillich's concept of the "God above God" rests on the inability of a finite being to know or define the infinite. So Tillich argues that the very statement "God *is*" is a theologically problematic one. The traditional notion of God as merely the *highest* being, thus sharing the same status with other "beings," is improper. Whatever the "is" means in "God is" cannot be the same kind of "is" that we mean when we say "this or that is." Accordingly, Tillich argued that God is not a being among other beings but rather "being-itself" or the "ground of being." God does not "exist" but is the ground of existence. Thus, God does not exist on the same plane of being as human beings or as any other created object; but instead, God is the source and ground of being itself. Thus, the problem of theology becomes: How can we describe, using only finite words, the source of all being, the uncreated and infinite Word? That establishes a sharp distinction between God as an object of human contemplation and the non-objectifiable "God above God." The former is speakable, and the latter is ineffable—or we might say "unnamable." As Tillich succinctly put it, "God transcends his own name."[5]

Negative theology necessarily presupposes the inadequacy of human speech in speaking about God; it assumes that for humans to speak of God is *to fail to speak of God.* But wouldn't that mean the end of theology? Perhaps it does mean the end of a particular *kind* of theology, namely, natural theologies, which tend to assume an easy point of contact between God and humankind. The most famous critic of natural theology was Karl Barth. By assuming that a finite mind *can* conceive of the infinite, natural theology is in some sense the opposite of negative theology—although this is not true for every natural theology. As Karl Barth argued, natural theology presupposes an *analogia entis* (analogy of being), which operates as a point of correspondence between our being and God's. Although Barth's theological program is in many ways the opposite of

Tillich, he nonetheless shares the fundamental conviction that God cannot become an object of human control, that God is non-objectifiable. Both Tillich and Barth share a dialectical impulse, though in very different ways. Barth wrote early in his career about the twofold obligation that we ought to speak of God (because God has spoken of Godself in Jesus Christ), yet we *cannot* speak of God adequately. This point is remarkably comparable to Beckett:

> As ministers we ought to speak of God. We are human, however, and cannot speak of God. We ought therefore to recognize both our obligation and our inability and by that very recognition give God the glory.[6]

We must speak of God, yet to speak as humans means to fail to speak of God. Barth aims to go beyond what is humanly possible—by grace. Similarly, Beckett aims to name the unnamable, to put nothingness into words. His artistic manifesto, which we first considered in the introduction, strives to transcend the "plane of the feasible" with, "The expression that there is nothing to express, nothing with which to express, nothing from which to express, no power to express, no desire to express, together with the obligation to express."[7] For Beckett, "to be an artist is to fail, as no other dare fail."[8] We might copy this famous artistic manifesto and use it to restate the task of theology: *To be a theologian is to fail to speak of God as no other dare fail.*

What drives Beckett's fidelity to failure? He wants to pierce language itself and get at whatever lies behind it. He made this claim in the context of explaining why he switched from writing in his native English to compose in French. He writes:

> It is indeed getting more and more difficult, even pointless, for me to write in formal English. And more and more my language appears to me like a veil which one has to tear apart in order to get to those things (or the nothingness) lying behind it. [...] To drill one hole after another into it until that which lurks behind, be it something or nothing, starts seeping through - I cannot imagine a higher goal for today's writer.[9]

Beckett compares language to a "mask" and longs for the day in which "language is best used where it is most efficiently abused."[10] This quest for that something or nothing behind words and beyond language is not a nihilistic escape from reality, but the search for a "beyond," for the "nothing" beyond things, i.e., for that which cannot be expressed in words and is thus transcendent, ineffable, and unnamable. It is the thing that is no longer a thing at all, or not merely, and a being that is no mere being. Beckett's quest is for "neither" being nor its absence, an unrelenting search for "unspeakable home." While Beckett does not equate this unspeakable home with God, his pursuit is uncannily similar to the mystic's quest. These points also share the logic of negative theology regarding God's ineffability. As Wynands realized, "Negative theology sees eye to eye with Beckett."[11] She explains:

> Beckett both produces and describes absolute irreducibility. His is both a mysticism and a theology of language. At the transcendental level of the literary Beckett creates a dark icon of the transcendent divine. Yet he is not able to affirm God [...] not yet: not God and not no God, but an open space in which he may give himself.[12]

Beckett's central literary obsession—the problem of having the speak yet being unable to—is prominent in all his work. The early short story "Assumption" is an example of how far-reaching this obsession was. The first line aptly describes Beckett's literary dilemma, "He could have shouted and could not."[13] This shout represents at once artistic fulfillment and divination. Thus, the "shout" perhaps recalls Stephen Dedalus' imminent vision of God as "a shout in the street."[14] Written at the age of twenty-three, "Assumption" explores the artist's quest and the deadly effect of trying to pursue both art and love. As the protagonist lies dead in the arms of his lover, the final image of the story evokes a strange sort of Pietá, of the dead Christ in the arms of Mary: "They found her caressing his wild dead hair."[15] Beckett links the protagonist's quest for artistic fulfillment with the pursuit of divinity: "Its struggle for divinity was as real as his own, and as futile."[16] The climax of the story—the artist's final release of a torrential scream that leaves him dead—is described theologically: "Thus each night he died and was God, each night revived and was torn, torn and battered with increasing grievousness, so that he hungered to be irretrievably engulfed in the light of eternity, one with the birdless cloudless colourless skies, in infinite fulfillment."[17] Beckett connects the pursuit of artistic fulfillment symbolically with the quest for mystical union with God. They are at least deeply intertwined, if not identical, pursuits.

The God whom Beckett rejects, according to Eugene Combs, is the domesticated God, the God we can name: "This 'God' is abhorrent to Beckett because he is definable, is knowable through the constructs of man's mind, is the 'creation' of man. The language about this God is man-made and refers only to the reality of man's constructs."[18] Yet there is a God beyond the domestic God, a non-objectifiable God, and it is this God whom the mystics pursue. As Combs continues, "Beckett is deeply conscious of Being that lies outside man and is beyond man, that is not knowable, but remains mystery."[19] Combs thinks Beckett attempts to "reinstate into modernity" an impenetrable sense of the divine with his art. The possibility of a God above God, of an unnamable Being beyond being itself, of an unnamable Word beyond words, is not unlike the object of Beckett's artistic quest. Perhaps it *is* the object of his quest, paradoxically. That is the argument of this chapter. Without explicitly being aware of this fact, Beckett's art is an unrelenting quest for truth and meaning and thus for the unnamable God.

Compare Beckett's artistic quest to how the mystic theologian Nilus Sorskij once described God: "God is 'a light that the world does not see,' something 'beyond speech and beyond words.'"[20] Theology's aim to speak of a God beyond speech and to use words to describe a God beyond words is the same quest Beckett goes on, only with a different vocabulary and goal. John Calder also realized this about Beckett, writing:

> All his work was in a sense a search for the God in which he did not believe except as a remote and indefinable possible presence, as well as a protest against the injustices that cover the planet with pain and misery and the creation of a self-created literary theology.[21]

Wynands, too, saw that "Beckett's absence of God signals, after all, the potential return of God."[22] On the other side of Beckett's protest against God, there is this passionate pursuit of a God beyond God. Whatever kind of God Beckett's work might signal a return to, it cannot be the domesticated, namable God of cheap spirituality. In terms similar to

Tillich's God above God, the God whom Beckett pursues is the God on the other side of doubt. Through the fires of unrelenting deconstruction —what is rightly called the death of God—the God that remains must be a God above God. In Beckett's God-haunted spaces, the weight of God's absence is not fundamentally atheistic. As I argued in the previous chapter, Beckett's literary atheism is atheism *for God's sake.* His work is not the absolute rejection of God but laments God's absence and quests for the God above God. Thus, the quest-motif is the other side of Beckett's protest atheism. In his unique way, Beckett was a literary mystic who traveled *via negativa* towards the affirmation of an unknown, ineffable divinity beyond being itself. His outlook is the same as the mystics, except he never goes so far as they do in attempting to name the unnamable; Beckett's God remains nameless.

Negative *theology*

For Moltmann, the *via negativa* is a necessary element in theology, although it must not become the negation of theology altogether. That is, it is negative *theology,* not *negative* theology. Without negative theology, God becomes an idol, something we grasp and control. The *via negativa* thus works as a corrective corollary to affirmative theology. It is rooted in the philosophical criticism of anthropomorphic talk of God and the Old Testament's prohibition of images. Beckett adopts a method similar to the theologians striving after an unspeakable God in his pursuit of the unnamable.

But there is a point of difference worth noting here. Moltmann affirms, following Barth, a dialectical method. We can only know God if God reveals God, and only then, according to *how* God reveals God. Thus, revelation is possible because God became a man in the incarnation. The finite cannot know the infinite, but if the infinite becomes finite, then God speaks of Godself in and to finitude. However, even in its givenness, revelation does not become an object of human control but remains God's revelation of Godself. Thus, divine revelation is an event of grace; we cannot know God apart from God. That is the entire basis for the Christian doctrine of God, not that we can speak of God but that God has spoken of Godself. *Deus dixit!* This affirmation highlights the chasm that still divides Beckett's relentless iconoclasm from theology's affirmation of God in Christ. Beckett is closer to *negative* theology, whereas theologians such as Moltmann are closer to negative *theology.*

In dialectical theology, revelation is not merely an abstract transfer of information from God to us. Instead, to know God is to be changed by God, to encounter God and repent. That explains why Barth stressed revelation and reconciliation as inseparable events. Moltmann continues from Barth and builds on his insights by stressing that God is known in Jesus Christ most of all through the event of the cross. If the cross was a God-event, then God's revelation is not without the suffering of God. He quotes an old Greek saying, "To know God means to suffer God."[23] So Moltmann realized, "The place where God encounters us, the *locus theologicus,* is the God-forsaken misery of the cross."[24] To know God is to struggle with God like Job and Jacob.

If revelation involves reconciliation (and vice versa); if we cannot know God without also being changed by God; and if this includes suffering God-forsakenness, then perhaps God is revealed in God's absence via the "dark night of the soul," which is sometimes called the eclipse of God. Moltmann notes how the most vivid Biblical revelations often took place during the times of greatest suffering and distress. One needs only mention the exodus and exile of Israel, which were foundational to the Hebraic concept of God. But most of all, it is through the suffering of Christ on the cross that God makes Godself known. Paradoxically, that means God is the most God-like when suffering and dying alone in weakness and God-forsakenness, and that we encounter God most directly by wrestling with God in daily life. That connects well with Moltmann's concept of the Spirit of Life that encounters us in the daily happenings of existence. God is not an object of abstraction, a thing we can grasp or control. Rather, God is an active being whom we engage and are engaged by, and thus, to know God is to struggle with God and against God—*for God.*

God in Christ entered God-forsaken spaces and made a home among the damned, lost, and forgotten. The paradox of Beckett's quest for nothingness, for the unword behind words, is not wholly devoid of God, nor is it nihilistic. We may read Beckett's artistic pursuit as the search for God despite the absence of God, as a quest to find God in God-forsakenness. Like St. John's "dark night of the soul"—a text we know Beckett read and was influenced by—we can conclude that his literary pursuit of failure is not anti-theological but profoundly theological. Of course, Beckett would likely reject this idea, but it is possible to read his work with a theological eye and see profound similarities even if he did not intend or plan them himself. A chasm remains between Beckett and theology, but his literary wrestling with God is profoundly spiritual. No quest for truth is devoid of God, ultimately, even the most seemingly atheistical. As we have seen, even atheism finds a home in the Christian faith through Christ's cry of protest from the cross.

Watt

Beckett's early novel *Watt* is about a man who tries to rationalize the irrational—with devastating results. By the end of the book, Watt cannot speak without inverting sentences, words, and letters into a jumbled mess of confusion. While his speech remains in the *shape* of rationality, the form of his speaking abstracts into absurdity. But for all the repetitions and convulsions of the novel, the book is also hilarious. It is such a strange literary experience, and for that reason, it is one of my favorite books by Beckett. At its core, it also shares similar impulses with negative theology and the mystical quest for God. It shares the logic of the spiritual rather than the rational. There is certainly a kind of rationality to the text, but there is a sense in which it is beyond logic. Thus, *Watt* fictionalizes the mystic's quest and puts into literary art a kind of spiritual logic. As Gottfried Büttner observed, "In *Watt* we find an inquiry into the very nature of human existence that is not afraid to enter areas inaccessible to rational thought."[25] Or, as Michael Robinson explained, "Beckett has rejected the power of reason and all claim to intellectual emminence and searched with a spiritual intensity for the presence that ought to be at the centre of the universe."[26] It is not quite right to label it a spiritual allegory (as Baldwin has) because even if it is that, it is not *only* that, but the spiritual parallels are too plentiful to ignore.

Watt is a book of unknowns. We sense that Beckett intended us to feel as confused as Watt feels throughout the text. But the "plot" (if it could even be called that) is relatively easy to describe. The mysterious Watt goes into the service of the infinitely more mysterious Mr. Knott. He moves through the ranks of the house until he is eventually replaced just as he replaced his predecessor. Watt leaves Mr. Knott's house in a state of disillusionment—or perhaps enlightenment?—and makes his way to a train station. He suffers a strange and humorous mishap, then boards the train. Watt somehow ends up in a mansion or large house with a garden, or perhaps it is an insane asylum, where he meets the book's narrator, Sam, who recounts his story. Yet this somewhat simplistic tale is obfuscated into oblivion with endless spiritualized rhetoric and mystical happenings.

When Watt reaches Mr. Knott's house, he finds that the front door is locked and the back door is locked. He re-checks them each in their turn, multiple times, and upon the third cycle of checking each door, the back door is suddenly and unexplainably open. He tries to understand this phenomenon intellectually, but the narrator concludes, "The result of this was that Watt never knew how he got into Mr. Knott's house."[27] Thus, Watt's journey in and through the house takes on a mystical tone from the start.

The oddities only continue as Watt's predecessor, Arsene, offers a "short statement" for his edification. Arsene first describes, again in quasi-mystical terms, the sounds of the house: "And all the sounds, meaning nothing [...] the little sounds come that demand nothing, ordain nothing, explain nothing, propound nothing."[28] That echoes how Beckett once described his writing to Alan Schneider: "My work is a matter of fundamental sounds (no joke intended), made as fully as possible, and I accept responsibility for nothing else."[29] Beckett frequently distanced himself from those aiming to discover some hidden meaning in his work. There is an artistic purity in this. Beckett did not have a lesson to teach or an ideological position to defend. He writes for the pure beauty of his art, but there remains such a depth of meaning that to ignore it altogether would be a mistake. So while Beckett always refused to explain his work, he did not forbid others from trying. As he continued, "If people want to have headaches among the overtones, let them. And provide their own aspirin."[30] Sounds meaning nothing are perhaps the most potent and meaning-evoking because they produce such profound overtones.

In his short statement, Arsene considers the question of want. The renouncement of wants is a common refrain in Christian mysticism. It is sometimes assumed that bodily needs and fleshly desires hinder union with God. This tendency to reject the body is theologically lamentable, but it is worth noting because it is a point that Beckett's work often echoed. Not only in *Watt* but throughout his texts, there is an apparent disdain for fleshly existence, which reflects the mystics' otherworldly aspirations. Arsene's statement, then, is a fine example of how Beckett mixes the mystics' desire for purity with his tragic-comic perspective:

> And yet it is useless not to seek, not to want, for when you cease to seek you start to find, and when you cease to want, then life begins to ram her fish and chips down your gullet until you puke, and then the puke down your gullet until you puke the puke, and then the puked puke until you begin to like it. The glutton castaway, the drunkard in the desert, the lecher in prison, they are the happy ones. To hunger, thirst, lust, everyday afresh and every day in vain, after the old prog, the old booze, the old whores, that's the nearest we'll ever get to felicity, the new porch and the very latest garden.[31]

True bliss is wanting what can never be satisfied, at least not on earth. To want and crave, to have a desire for something and a haunting memory of its absence, but with no hope of ever finding fulfillment; that is Arsene's vision of happiness. Now consider Augustine's famous prayer from the *Confessions*, which echoes similar disdain for fleshly desires: "But what do I love when I love my God? Not material beauty or beauty of a temporal order; not the brilliance of earthy light, so welcome to our eyes..."[32] He goes on to list the things he does not love in loving God, such as melody, flowers, smells, food, spices, etc. Rather, for Augustine, the object of his love for God goes beyond the bodily and takes the form of spiritual senses. He turns inward rather than outward to find God. The desire to forgo the things of the flesh, to no longer need or seek or want, is an underlying drive here. Want not the things of this earth but the things above. Arsene affirms the impossibility of wanting nothing, and concludes instead that to want, but to be unable to fulfill said want, is the height of bliss. Thus, it is a kind of mystical hunger, a striving after the unnamable, intangible no-thingness—for the thing beyond things.

Later in his short speech, Arsene utters one of the best-written passages of the book, from which I quote a small part:

> Personally of course I regret everything. Not a word, not a deed, not a thought, not a need, not a grief, not a joy, not a girl, not a boy, not a doubt, not a trust, not a scorn, not a lust, not a hope, not a fear, not a

> smile, not a tear, not a name, not a face, no time, no place, that I do not regret, exceedingly. An ordure, from beginning to end.[33]

This recalls Kierkegaard's character Aesthete, who famously reflected on regret, "Do it, or do not do it—you will regret it either way."[34] But above all, Beckett's poetic musicality is on brilliant display in this passage, and it only continues to shine as Arsene goes on:

> The Tuesday scowls, the Wednesday growls, the Thursday curses, the Friday howls, the Saturday snores, the Sunday yawns, the Monday morns, the Monday morns. The whacks, the moans, the cracks, the groans, the welts, the squeaks, the belts, the shrieks, the pricks, the prayers, the kicks, the tears, the skelps, and the yelps. And the poor old lousy old earth, my earth and my father's and my mother's and my father's father's and my mother's mother's and my father's mother's and my mother's father's and my father's mother's father's and my mother's father's mother's [...][35]

Words become music. Here the "fundamental sounds" of Beckett's art are evident. But it is not merely an aesthetic decision. What are sounds and music but an expression beyond words? Arsene's statement continues until we stumble upon a profoundly mystical declaration: "what we know partakes in no small measure of the nature of what has so happily been called the unutterable and ineffable, so that any attempt to utter or eff it is doomed to fail, doomed, doomed to fail."[36] That reinforces the idea that Watt has left the realm of the possible and entered the spiritual world of unnamable and ineffable thingless things. Thus, it is a story of mystical ascent, of one man who stumbled into a world beyond the rational. It is possible, then, to read it as a spiritual quest for the divine. The musicality of the text further supports the sense of a mystical quest. At one point, even the frogs have a chorus to sing. Beyond the possible and speakable realms, there is the realm of music, which is perhaps the closest logical alternative to mysticism.

Arsene leaves, and Watt is left alone in his confusion, "Watt did not know what to think."[37] Watt's work in Mr. Knott's house begins on the ground floor, where he has no direct dealings with Mr. Knott. The narrator cryptically reflects, "Not that Watt was ever to have any direct dealings with Mr. Knott, for he was not."[38] That alludes to the idea that Mr. Knott is a wholly-other, transcendent no-thingness beyond being itself, whom one can never deal with directly. We cannot directly deal with the divine because it would no longer be divinity if we could. A God we can hold in our hands or grasp fully with our intellect is, by definition, no God at all.[39] Knott is a kind of void in the center of the house like God is a kind of void in creation—at once ever-present and absent because beyond being and non-being.

Watt is often trying to make sense of that which is beyond sense and nonsense alike, and he explicitly connects this quest with God's ineffability. Just as one must speak of nothing only as if it were something, so one must speak of God only as if a man. This comparison parodies the traditional, philosophical approach to God, which places divinity as the highest good of humanity. Watt reflects:

> For the only way one can speak of nothing is to speak of it as though it were something, just as the only way one can speak of God is to speak of him as though he were a man, which to be sure he was, in a sense, for a time, and as the only way one can speak of man, even our anthropologist have realized that, is to speak of him as though he were a termite.[40]

Another vital scene highlights Watt's failure to rationalize the irrational: a piano tuner and his son tune the piano. But Watt simply cannot comprehend this basic act. He is unable to accept that "nothing had happened, with all the clarity and solidity of something."[41] It disturbs Watt greatly. "But he could not accept it, could not bear it."[42] The narrator explains, "Watt learned towards the end of this stay in Mr. Knott's house to accept that nothing had happened, that a nothing had happened, learned to bear it and even, in a shy way, to like it."[43] Nothing happened as if it were something, and Watt cannot come to terms with it. That is arguably *the* premise of *Watt*: nothing happens with the force or shape of something. Thus, it is a kind of mystical striving for the impossible, to go beyond things and no-things in speaking of nothing as if it were something, God as if a man.

Mr. Knott's not-ness sets him apart as a figure of the divine. God's absence is not pure nothingness, but rather a no-thing that has the fullness of a some-thing, of an ineffable event. This conviction is central to mystical theology. God is most present in the "dark night of the soul," in God-forsakenness. God is the hidden God; nothing is more real than no-thing. No-thingness here meaning the thing beyond things, the being that is not being but the ground of being, to use Tillich's phrase. Mr. Knott is an apt representative of the divine (whether or not he is meant to represent the divine or is himself divinity) because Mr. Knott is a forceful nothingness that has the form and shape of something. And this means he transcends his very presence. In theological terms, the absence of God is often more profound than God's presence because only a God who could transcend God's own presence could genuinely be a God above God. Beckett's insight is profound, whether he realized the connection here or not. God must be beyond God to be God at all; God must transcend God's being, be "no-thing" with the clarity and solidity of some-thing. Only as such is God genuinely divine rather than a mere projection of humanity's best thoughts.

Beckett describes Mr. Knott as if he were God. That is not on account of his presence but precisely because of his absence, just as negative theology affirms God not for what God is but what God is not. Mr. Knott's name is a giveaway for the "not-ness" of divinity, the inability of human, finite speech to "name" God. Whether we read this to mean the absence of God or, in Tillich's phrase, as pointing to the God above God, it remains a profound image. The symbolism is clear. Mr. Knott is likely not God, but he is not *not* God. He is thus a proto-Unnamable in Beckett's canon.

Consider the many similarities between how Beckett describes Knott and how theology describes God: Mr. Knott is without want (perfect, lacking nothing), he is immobile, like an unmoved and unmovable oak (the unmoved mover), he rests on the seventh day (Sabbath), the furniture in his room revolves around him (much like the sun), he is called a "harbour" and "haven," he radiates a "fascia of white light," he eats fish on Fridays (at least the fishwife calls on Thursdays), and Beckett describes him as if he were impassible and eternal. In addition to these similarities, Beckett's language in *Watt* feels sacramental. He often uses words and phrases with either a Biblical or spiritual origin, such as "witness," "abide," "transgression," "forgive," "mansion," "first was last," "turn the other cheek," etc.

Mr. Knott and his home are wrapped in mystery. That is perhaps why

Watt cannot rationalize anything he experienced at Mr. Knott's establishment: finite beings cannot comprehend the infinite. While it is doubtful that Beckett had a religious allegory in mind with Mr. Knott, it is hard to ignore the parallels. And in this sense, Watt's quest is comparable to the mystics' search for God. Indeed, the narrator tells us that "Watt suffered neither from the presence of Mr. Knott, nor from his absence."[44] What is beyond presence and absence? Only divinity transcends nothing and something, being and non-being. Thus, Watt is a mystic struggling through the dark night of the soul, experiencing at once God's absence and presence.

Watt's quest may be a failure (although Baldwin argues for its success), but it is a quest with mystical aims. Whatever or whomever Mr. Knott represents, it is unmistakable that Beckett describes him as a deity and that Watt has gone mad trying to understand him and his strange kingdom. An important example, yet again linking Watt's quest to the mystics, is a picture Watt finds hanging in Erskine's room (which hangs "on a nail," alluding to Christ crucified). The image is a black circle on a white background. The circle is open at its lowest point, and there is a blue dot appearing to recede in the background. Hélène Baldwin calls it an "icon representing God,"[45] and she notes that St. Augustine and Julian of Norwich used a similar image. The image represented, for them, a definition of God whose "circumference is nowhere and whose center is everywhere."[46] It indicates God's omnipresence and ineffability. God is everywhere present, nowhere contained, and cannot be defined by finite beings. The image tries to say what we cannot say with finite words. It is an icon of negative theology. Watt is brought to tears as he reflects on the image and its implications of "boundless space" and "endless time" (attributes of divinity often posited by negation). The presence of this image and its link to mystical theology only reinforces the point that Beckett intends to establish Mr. Knott as a mystical figure.

With *Watt,* Beckett shows the absurdity of knowing the infinite in and through the finite, a central conviction of negative theology. His exhaustive (and hilariously absurd) lists of names, movements, and possibilities maximize this principle and its futility, such as the attempt to describe Mr. Knott's movements in his room. Only a portion of this will suffice to see the connection: "Here he moved, to and fro, from the door to the window, from the window to the door; from the window to the door, from the door to the window; from the fire to the bed, from the bed to the fire; from the bed to the fire, from the fire to the bed; from the door to the fire…"[47] And so on and on. This list of Mr. Knott's movements goes on for an entire page, and it is just one of many examples of such attempts to describe or explain the impossible. But this particular description is noteworthy because it seems to be a literary equivalent of the picture from Erskine's room. It tries to describe a being without circumference or fixed center, boundless space and endless time.

I do not mean to imply that *Watt* is entirely a religious allegory, but it is an excellent example of how Beckett intertwines mystical and philosophical ideas into his art. He does not seem to use them to argue a particular theological point, but they give a unique shape to his literary endeavor. The mystics' quest begins with the acceptance of ignorance, the embrace of the failure of speaking of God, and it thus strives after a "third way" beyond denying or affirming God in human terms. It is the way of silence and ignorance, which echoes Nicholas of Cusa's mystical description of theology as "learned ignorance." To be a theologian is to fail to speak of God as none failed before. Beckett's literary quest operates on remarkably similar lines of thought. Thus, *Watt* bears witness to the profound spiritual sensibilities at the core of his art.

Molloy

Molloy is another text that relies heavily on the themes of negative theology and the mystic's quest. There is even a direct allusion to negative theology similar to the one found in *Watt*. Molloy remembers his love for anthropology and reflects, "What I liked in anthropology was its inexhaustible faculty of negation, its relentless definition of man, as though he were no better than God, in terms of what he is not."[48] A casual reader may miss the hint, but it is a clear allusion to negative theology. Man is no better than God: he is known by what he is not.

Another aspect of *Molloy* that lends itself to a mystical reading is Beckett's description of several events that can only be called spiritual ecstasies. Baldwin even went so far as to consider the novel a "religious allegory."[49] She identified five passages that express a mystical experience. The third of these examples is, in my estimation, the most beautiful, so I quote it in full. It involves the paradoxical description of a soundless, timeless place, or perhaps a vision of the end of the world:

> I listen and the voice is of a world collapsing endlessly, a frozen world, under a faint untroubled sky, enough to see by, yes, and frozen too. And I hear it murmur that all wilts and yields, as if loaded down, but here and there are no loads, and the ground too, unfit for loads, and the light too, down towards an end it seems can never come. For what possible end to these wastes where true light never was, nor any upright thing, nor any true foundation, but only these leaning things, forever lapsing and crumbling away, beneath a sky without memory of morning or hope of night.[50]

Another mystical example follows soon after. It is a moment of self-forgetting, the paradoxical bliss of union with the earth, and the unmaking of the self. Thus, it is an example of striving after transcendence:

> And there was another noise, that of my life become the life of this garden as it rode the earth of deeps and wildernesses. Yes, there were times when I forgot not only who I was, but that I was, forgot to be. Then I was no longer that sealed jar to which I owed my being so well preserved, but a wall gave way and I filled with roots and tame stems [...] then the labour of the planet rolling eager into winter, winter would rid it of these contemptible scabs.[51]

"After reading this passage perhaps a hundred times," writes Ruby Cohn, "I do not pretend to understand it, but I feel it."[52] Both examples have an emotional effect, but at their core, they indicate a mystical bend to Molloy's quest. Molloy admits that such experiences are rare, "But that did not happen to me often, mostly I stayed in my jar."[53] "Jar" refers to Molloy's finite body, which, in a kind of union with nature (with infinity), he escapes for a brief moment and becomes one with the earth and its timelessness. I cannot help but think of Schleiermacher's famous definition of religion and eternity here. In the nineteenth century, he wrote that "true religion is sense and taste for the infinite."[54] Or consider his longer description, "To seek and to find this infinite and eternal factor in all that lives and moves, in all growth and change, in all action and passion, and to have and to know life itself only in immediate feeling—that is religion."[55] While Schleiermacher's definition is not uncontroversial, it sheds light on Molloy's experience.

But beyond these mystical episodes, Molloy's spiritual sensibilities are clear from the beginning of the novel. At one point, he reflects on "the sky where without seeing them I felt the first stars tremble."[56] Unseeing, that is, beyond the function of fleshly eyes, Molloy communes with the infinite and feels the stars tremble. Experiences of coming out of this state of self-forgetting are also present. He returns to his jar and comes upon the sudden but strange realization he is still alive: "I am still alive then. That may come in useful."[57] Even Molloy's remembrance of imminent death is accepted stoically: "It is in the tranquillity of decomposition that I remember the long confused emotion which was my life, and that I judge it, as it is said that God will judge me, and with no less impertinence."[58]

Explicitly religious imagery is often present as well. Molloy has resolved to go and see his mother. On the way, he is stopped by a policeman, momentarily forgets his name (another instance of mystical self-forgetting), and is told to move on for the sake of "public decency." Social workers present him with a quasi-Eucharistic offering of tea and stale bread, but he flings it away, commenting: "To him who has nothing it is forbidden not to relish filth."[59] He takes out a pebble from his pocket and begins to suck it, the smoothness of which "appeases, soothes, makes you forget your hunger, forget your thirst."[60] Molloy's poverty and status as a social outcast allude to Christ-likeness. Beckett evokes Christ directly when Molloy sees a boatman with a group of donkeys carrying a load of timber and nails. The Christian symbolism is unmistakable. The boatman had a "long white beard," and Molloy reflects that perhaps the timber and nails were on their way to "some carpenter." Christ, the carpenter, rode into Jerusalem on a donkey to be nailed to a cross. The boatman perhaps represents God the Father, preparing the timber and nails. Molloy then lays down in the grass in a cross-like posture, "with outspread arms." A bird—perhaps symbolizing the resurrection or, just as likely, another cruciform shape—flies overhead.

Molloy tries to ride his bicycle (a difficult task with bad knees) and runs over a dog. In a comical turn, the dog's owner was just on her way to euthanize the animal, but Molloy beat her to it. After her initial anger, she comes to see that Molloy saved her the trouble. But the least he could do is help bury the dog, although Molloy ends up being useless for the task. Lousse or Sophie, he isn't sure what her name is, takes Molloy into her home, where he is cared for. In this sense, Molloy takes the place of the dog he killed.

At Lousse's house, the two mystical experiences quoted above take place. In captivity, Molloy reflects on freedom. He first considers, somewhat comically, "Can it be we are not free? It might be worth looking into."[61] Molloy alludes to Arnold Geulincx in the text. He was a post-cartesian, flemish philosopher often linked with occasionalism, and someone Beckett seems to have been fascinated with. The occasionalists thought that all events are caused directly by God. If I want to lift a pen from the table in front of me, I can only do so because God directly causes it to happen.[62] It is a kind of extreme determinism that is of little philosophical or theological merit on its own. Yet, Beckett's use of it is noteworthy because of its mystical overtones. For the occasionalist, all is miraculous because all activity is the activity of the divine.

Molloy, reflecting on freedom, remembers an image from Geulincx of a man on the boat Ulysses, heading West. Yet, the "free" man is permitted to crawl eastward. This paradox aims to express how freedom is always relative to the will of God. Thus, his point is that nothing in the world matters but God. Any action that does not pursue union with God is futile. Beckett's description of the slave crawling on the boat feels almost spiritual, or at least poetic: "And from the poop, poring upon the wave, a sadly rejoicing slave, I follow with my eyes the proud and futile wake. Which, as it bears me from no fatherland away, bears me onward to no shipwreck."[63] There is a sense of comfort in knowing that whatever he does, no matter how badly he fails, he floats along the correct path because he is not free to do otherwise.

Molloy finally leaves Lousse's house, but it is not until a "small voice" implores him, "Get out of here, Molloy."[64] That is a clear allusion to God's "still small voice" when speaking to Elijah (1 Kings 19:11-13). A policeman stops Molloy and asks what he is doing, "a question to which I have never been able to find the correct reply."[65] These examples reinforce Geulincx's influence, especially the idea that only what is of God counts. The dualism is familiar to Beckett's literature, as humanity is frequently resigned to the mud of their existence, and all that's left of divinity is but a distant, impassible determinism. Thus, Molloy's ignorance of what he is doing is akin to the mystics' surrender to the will of God. He listens not to himself but the "small voice."

Simone Weil, for example, in her collection of letters and essays, *Waiting for God*, talks about her obedience to God in a way not unlike Geulincx: "I have always regarded myself as a slave;"[66] And elsewhere, "It concerns God. I am really nothing in it all."[67] Weil was an interesting figure who professed she lived "at the intersection of Christian and everything that is not Christianity."[68] Her devotion to God was that of a mystic-philosopher, an outsider-saint. "It is not my business to think about myself," she writes, "My business is to think about God. It is for God to think about me."[69] Her obedience to God was so extreme that she once even confessed that if God willed for her to go into the center of hell and stay there forever, she would do it.[70] While she accepted the possibility of rebellion, which Geulincx's fatalism does not, she nevertheless aspired to a similar vision of living the wholly God-controlled life. Molloy refers to life in similar fatalistic terms, "And the cycle continues, joltingly, of flight and bivouac, in an Egypt without bounds, without infant, without mother."[71]

Weil is not an accidental example. I bring her up not only because she helps explain the mystical elements of Beckett's novel but because of two interesting, biographical possibilities. Her posthumous collection of essays and letters, *Attente de Dieu* (published in 1950, three years before *Godot*), bears an unmistakable resemblance to *En Attendant Godot.* Direct influence is unlikely, but both Weil and Beckett lived in Paris around the same time. The likelihood of their familiarity grows when we remember Beckett taught at the École Normale Superieure while Weil attended as a student (1928-1930). She was a gifted academic, and so it is unlikely that Beckett was not, at the very least, aware of her.

Another oddity is that both Beckett and Weil worked in the French Resistance, even though they likely never crossed paths. Baldwin wrote to Beckett to ask about the connection, but he denied knowing her and admitted he was "little acquainted with her works."[72] For Beckett, who once denied that he had ever read philosophers (a massive lie), to admit that he was "little acquainted with her works" is tantamount to saying that he had likely read something from her. At the very least, it is hard to write it off as nothing. We might conclude that he at least knew of her and perhaps even read her. It is possible that Weil's book influenced the title of *Waiting for Godot,* but whether consciously or unconsciously, it is impossible to say.

But setting aside biographical speculation, there is a more substantial similarity between Beckett and Weil: their relentless pursuit of the truth and passionate refusal of all systems and certainties standing in the way. Weil writes, tellingly:

> For it seemed to me certain, and I still think so today, that one can never wrestle enough with God if one does so out of pure regard for the truth. Christ likes us to prefer truth to him because, before being Christ, he is truth.[73]

As previously argued, Beckett, like Bloch, was an "atheist for God's sake," an individual who refused to accept cheap faith and wrestled continually with God, protesting against God in the name of God and for the sake of the truth. That, too, was Weil's conviction, and she remained outside the traditional boundary-lines of faith all her life because of it. She never joined the Church formally, nor was she ever baptized. As Leslie A. Fiedler writes, "[Weil] teaches the uncomfortable truth that the unbelief of many atheists is closer to a true love of God and a true sense of his nature, than the kind of easy faith which, never having *experienced* God, hangs a label bearing his name on some childish fantasy or projection of the ego."[74] A better description of Beckett's relationship to religion and faith would be hard to find.

After listening to the small voice and fleeing Lousse's house, Molloy reflects on the peace of unknowing: "For to know nothing is nothing, not to want to know anything likewise, but to be beyond knowing anything, to know you are beyond knowing anything, that is when peace enters in, to the soul of the incurious seeker."[75] He also thinks about the unbearable brevity of life. At one point he hyperbolizes the absurdity of life and compares himself to "one dying of cancer obliged to consult his dentist."[76] He grieves that life is indeed like Shakespeare's "brief candle," it is a light "doomed no sooner lit to be extinguished."[77] Elsewhere, Molloy compares life to a "veritable calvary, with no limit to its stations, and no hope of crucifixion."[78] These are all familiar themes in Beckett's writing.

Mystics often reflect on both tendencies: the peaceful acceptance of unknowing and the imminent approach of death, *memento mori* (together with *ars moriendi,* the art of dying). From the beginning of the novel, Molloy expresses his wish to "speak of the things that are left, say my goodbyes, finish dying."[79] Death is never far from Beckett's characters, but this obsession, rather than succumbing to nihilism, is closer to the Church's ancient call to "remember death." Even though Molloy seems to fear that death is "a state of being even worse than life,"[80] he cannot help but contemplate its imminence.

Molloy's quest ends in a forest. After killing a man he presumed to be a "coal-burner," Molloy crawls through the woods until his strength gives out. He then hears a voice, more clearly than before, almost audible: "I heard a voice telling me not to fret, that help was coming [...] we're coming."[81] So the novel ends with Molloy at the bottom of a ditch, listening to a voice promising rescue. He hears birds flying above and contemplates how he has not heard them in a long time. It must be spring, he reasons. Baldwin reads these two images (birds and spring) as symbols of resurrection. We know Molloy eventually ends up in his mother's room, but we do not know how. Thus, Molloy's story seems to end at a point of rebirth. But it has unmistakably mystical overtones because we do not know the how or why or who of his arrival home. And Moran's quest hardly fills in the details.

The second half of *Molloy* follows the quest of Moran. It is, in many ways, the opposite of Molloy's quest. Moran begins as a self-righteous and self-assured (though hypocritical) religious man and ends as one who has lost all sense of certainty, even the confidence of the self and reality. He goes to find Molloy and, in a sense, becomes him.

Biblical figures immediately abound in Moran's story. Gaber, a name reminiscent of the chief angel Gabriel, relays a message from Youdi, which sounds a bit like the Hebraic name for God, YHWH. And in the background, Moran's housemaid Martha prepares lunch (see Luke 10:38-42). Moran misses mass to meet with Gaber and takes, in private, the Eucharist with Father Ambrose. Moran is religious but not serious. His inner monologue seems to suggest a passive, inherited religiosity rather than a personally reverent one. It remains external rather than internal.

This kind of religiosity is perhaps not unlike Beckett's upbringing; his mother May was deeply religious. From what we can gather, she was also about as harsh with Beckett as Moran is with his son.

Moran's thoughts often return to religious and theological concerns. He muses about plants and sees in them "a superfetatory proof of the existence of God."[82] At one point, however, he admits to being comforted by God's silence: "I asked the Lord for guidance. Without result. That was some consolation."[83] He wonders if the beer he shared with Gaber counted as a meal before Eucharist, forbidden by the Catholic faith, but he takes it anyway. The neighbor dog annoys him, and with this, Moran's thoughts take another revealing turn, "I don't like men and I don't like animals. As for God, he is beginning to disgust me."[84]

Moran's quest leads him into the woods, where he begins to take on the same characteristics as Molloy: his legs become stiff, and he can no longer recognize his reflection; he even kills a man (who at first looks like him) for no reason and in the same manner that Molloy killed the man at the end of his journey. His son leaves the first chance he gets, and Moran finds himself abandoned, crippled, and confused. His mind wanders, and he begins to lapse into a kind of insanity. He undergoes the loss of self and identity. As Moran descends further into the quest of unmaking himself, he adopts a semi-mystical posture towards his body. He comically longs for total paralysis:

> To be literally incapable of motion at last, that must be something! My mind swoons when I think of it. And mute into the bargain! And perhaps as deaf as a post! And who knows as blind as a bat! And as likely as not your memory a blank! And just enough brain intact to allow you to exult! And to dread death like regeneration.[85]

That may be an expression of the death-drive, as Moran later reflects, "I lay down on the ground near the fire and fell asleep, saying, Perhaps a spark will set fire to my clothes and I wake a living torch."[86] But it is also not unlike the bodily disdain that traditional mysticism often evoked. For example, consider the tradition of self-flagellation in some parts of the Catholic world. It also seems to reflect a desire for self-transcendence. Indeed, Moran's transformation is so radical that he no longer recognizes himself; he accepts a "growing resignation to being dispossessed of self."[87]

Earlier, Moran sensed that his life is spiraling into madness, "I could not understand what was happening to me. […] I tried to pull myself together. In vain. […] My life was running out, I knew not through which breach."[88] His religious certainties begin to slip away as well. Moran's story spirals from assurance and respectability to doubt and the loss of self. This journey is not unlike the deconstruction of faith that many go through in life. It involves stripping away preconceived, unquestioned ideals and facing up against brute reality. It consists of the eclipse of God and the experience of God-forsakenness. Moran's faith was shallow from the beginning, and its loss is thus only the shedding of falsity, but he follows the same trajectory of those who struggle and question their faith, especially naive childhood faiths. I can attest to this first hand, as someone who grew up in the Church. But while my faith has been deconstructed countless times since leaving home, what remains is not faithlessness but a more profound, robust expression of that authentic faith. Beyond the cheap faith we give ourselves, there is a faith that withstands even the most severe deconstruction.

Moran's deconstruction comes to a head with a list of theological questions that have preoccupied his mind in the woods. Only someone with a keen awareness of theological issues could have written this list. They include common problems like whether Mary conceived through the ear, as Augustine and Abelard thought, and what God was doing with himself before creation. They also involve more obscure questions, such as what to make of the "algebraic theology of Craig" and if we should approve of the Italian cobbler Lovat who dismembered and crucified himself. Only Beckett would know or care to remember someone so obscure as John Craig, a Scottish mathematician who applied probability to show that the truth of the Gospels would slowly diminish through time until reaching 0 in the year 3144, which he then considered the limit of Christ's second coming. The two attempted self-crucifixions of Mattio Lovat are another forgotten oddity of history. Only recently (2018) has someone published a book about this strange event.[89] Lovat's case was one of religious insanity and points to religion's sad tendency to prey on the mentally ill. But it fits Moran's spiral into self-forgetting and madness. A final theological question highlights Moran's growing paralysis: "What if the mass for the dead were read over the living?"[90]

Like Molloy, Moran hears a voice: "I have spoken of a voice giving me orders, or rather advice. It was on the way home I heard it for the first time." But unlike Molloy, Moran "paid no attention to it."[91] A full year after setting out, Moran finally returns home. The final scene expresses at once Moran's madness and the deconstruction of his story, self, and sense of reality: "Then I went into the house and wrote, It is midnight. The rain is beating on the windows. It was not midnight. It was not raining."[92] Thus, in a twist, the story from start to finish is like a snake consuming its own tail. We can no longer trust anything Moran has written. The mystical quest for nothingness is (seemingly) realized, the desire to say nothing as if it were something.

Overall, Moran's quest is unique in Beckett's literature. He is one of the few characters to undergo such a radical and total deconstruction of the self. To some extent, all of his characters go through a similar experience, but not with such severity. Perhaps not by mistake, Moran's first name, rarely evoked, is Jacques. One of the central voices in deconstructionism is Jacques Derrida. Most of Beckett's characters begin where Moran ends, including Molloy. But here, we see the spiral from beginning to end. In this sense, we may read it as a fictionalization of the deconstruction of faith and certainty, perhaps even alluding to Beckett's own loss of faith. Deconstruction is in many ways akin to the dark night of the soul in the mystics or the eclipse of God in Tillich and modern theology. We could also call it the death of God. Moran suffers the death of God and the loss of his faith and his very identity as a result. Modernity has suffered the same fate. And what remains is either the total loss of faith and God or something beyond the cheap certainties we once held dear. As a literary expression of deconstruction, Beckett's Moran paradoxically points to the need for a God after the death of God. Just as Moltmann has written that the death of God on the cross is either the end of theology or its complete renewal, so Moran's story is either the end of literature and words or its augmentation to some unnamable beyond. And this is where Beckett takes us, through Moran and Molloy, into the world of Malone and the Unnamable.

Happy Days

Happy Days is Beckett's most memorable use of dramatic irony. It is not a happy day. Instead, it is a play that tells of what happens when all hope for happy days has disappeared. Accordingly, the critic Alfred Simon considered the death of God a central theme in *Happy Days.* It thus tells a similar tale as Moran's downward spiral in *Molloy,* of the loss of self and certainty in the loss of God. Simon explains, in response to Catholic critics who called the play blasphemous:

> The pessimistic vision of Beckett has nothing partial, systematic, or arbitrary about it. It is merely untenable. And here is the tragic paradox of Beckett: he affirms the untenable. Sartre said that life begins on the other side of despair. For the believer in our time, faith begins after the death of God [...] We must return to the very foundation of tragedy as it was perceived by the Greeks: the confrontation between and evil God and human Freedom in revolt: the wickedness of God and the revolt of man each being implied by the other. What is the meaning of Winnie on her bare mound? What is the meaning of Job on his heap of ashes, and of Prometheus on his rock? [...] The evil God weighs heavy upon Beckett's universe [...] Samuel Beckett has steeped himself in the death of God.[93]

Death of God theology became a way to express the eclipse of God in the aftermath of modern tragedies. It refers more to the end of certainty than it does to the end of God. As Tillich argued, it is the God above God that remains in the ashes of the death of God.

Happy Days uses irony and dark humor to show the decay of a religious and respectable woman coming to terms with her fatal, inescapable condition. Winnie is buried up to her waist in act I, then neck in act II. She exists under a blistering ray of heat, and she is daily forced awake by a loud ringing. Beckett's love for Dante is on display here. The play feels like a kind of torturous purgatory. Under unending torment, Winnie begins to lose grip on the sense of self and certainty she once held dear. She quotes not only religious texts but cultural and literary ones. Critics have often noted that this play is one of Beckett's most literary, but functionally, these allusions work to show the loss of self and certainty while trying to keep up the facade.

In this light, Simon's reading of the play as an expression of the death of God is plausible. Either the world itself is in a state of apocalyptic hopelessness, or Winnie herself is in purgatory. But in both cases, she is forced to come to terms with the cheap certainties she once found comforting, which no longer hold any weight. Her words echo hollowly, and the irony is palpable—and often very funny. The play operates as an iconoclastic response to the cultural and religious norms, the so-called respectable ideas of society, both literary and religious, not to mention its naive optimism. Winnie's relationship with Willie is perhaps a skeptical statement on modern love and its popular romanticization. And her fixation with things is comparable to the commodity fetishism of modern capitalism. Yet none of these falsities bring her any real comfort, or so it seems. The overall "strangeness" of the play, which Beckett highlights as its "necessary condition," seems to point to the strangeness of respectable society and religiosity. It is strange precisely in its familiarity. We are not unlike Winnie when we play the part of respectable people in an unrespectable world, holding fast to our things and traditions as if these make us human.

The death of God in the individual is often experienced much like this. We are lead to doubt that Winnie believes, or if believing not sincerely, any of what she is saying. Such is the crisis of faith, which is always a communal phenomenon. Those who undergo the death of God in their own lives are often left in the odd position to still play the part while inwardly struggling with doubt. But when those words that once brought comfort are gone, empty and dead, what remains is closer to the true and the real than what we once held onto. The death of God is not the end of theology but its entrance into something deeper and fuller, to a more Christ-like God. Even Christ experienced the death of God in His cry from the cross—a literary cry, like Winnie's, since it comes from Psalms 22—"My God, my God, why have you forsaken me?" Yet after death—resurrection.

Conclusion

Samuel Beckett was relentless in his quest for truth, but it ends in failure and oblivion. Yet, that is precisely why it is so profound. He sought a truth beyond naming, beyond philosophies and dogmas and creeds, a truth which we will always fail to name with words. As Avigdor Arikha said of Beckett, "All he wants is to tell the truth. That might be crazy in the last quarter of the 20th century, but truth is timeless [...] I do not exaggerate when I say that is what his writing is all about. He questions everything. His writing is a perpetual questioning of what is true."[94] Beckett's quest is the way of the mystic, to speak the unspeakable and pierce through the veil of false certainties to that which is beyond human control. His quest may not see eye to eye with what we commonly call "faith" (where faith = certainty), but his unceasing search has more in common with true faith than not. True faith means wrestling with God and truth and never settling for cheap substitutes. Honest doubting and continual questioning are a part of faith because faith includes the refusal to accept "cheap" certainty, the kind of certainty we might give ourselves.

Christian faith must resist the temptations of cheap faith and remain in pursuit of the unattainable; we must remember that faith is a pilgrimage, and we have not yet arrived at that unspeakable home. Simplistic answers cannot domesticate the chaos of existence. Just as Watt tried to rationalize the categorically irrational—or perhaps it was not irrational, but the ineffable, unnamable Other—so faith pursues the impossible task of knowing and naming the unnamable God. Christian faith today must reject cheap faith and thus learn to be okay with unanswerable questions. As the theoretical physicist Richard Feynman once said, "It is better to have questions we cannot answer than answers we cannot question."

A theological appreciation of Samuel Beckett cannot help but marvel at his literary courage to relentlessly pursue the unknown, to refuse to settle for empty solutions, to renounce all dogmatic certainty, and to search on unceasingly for the unspeakable home. While the theologian of grace will rightly assert that it is ultimately God who finds the human subject, who takes up the burden of pursuing us, it is also precisely because God seeks us that we seek God in turn. And even though the grace of God grasps us, that does not free us from human weakness and finitude; it is *because* we have felt the touch of grace that the quest goes on. As Augustine heard God say, "Take heart; you would not be seeking Me if I had not already found You."

Christian theology is *theologia viatorum*, a "theology of pilgrims." It never claims to have arrived but remains ever on the way. Honest faith is unsatisfied with false certainty and goes on pursuing, seeking, stirring still the weary way towards truth. Beckett's unceasing quest does not merely parallel the quest of faith. In many ways, it *is* a quest of faith. He may not arrive at the same conclusion (because he doubts more fiercely), but he is on the same path.

Karl Barth, who wrote what is arguably the lengthiest single work of dogmatic theology in the history of the Christian Church, understood theology to be the theology of pilgrims. The nine-thousand pages of his *Church Dogmatics* may give the illusion of having "arrived," but Barth did not see it like that. Instead, he writes that "theology can *only* be a *theologia viatorum*."[95] And therefore, "Faith refuses to grasp after any axioms and guarantees. Faith knows that man cannot comfort himself; that comfort [...] is the work of God."[96] That is what I'm trying to say with Beckett. This same refusal to accept dogmatic certainty, the refusal to be comforted by cheap axioms or guarantees, is central to Beckett's literary quest for the unnamable. It is only God who, in grace, grants the comfort of faith. But faith is always a *comfort in uncertainty* and *not*, as fundamentalism would have us believe, *the removal of uncertainty*. We cannot find comfort in ourselves; the only certainty is *God's* certainty, a gift of grace. Only the comfort God provides in uncertainty is enough.

Thus, faith and doubt are not mutually exclusive; in fact, they are necessary companions. Paul Tillich recognized this, writing that "serious doubt is confirmation of faith. It indicates the seriousness of the concern, its unconditional character."[97] Faith must include a serious doubt, if it is faith at all. Faith and doubt need each other. As I have stressed, both sides of the fundamentalist spectrum—dogmatic theism and atheism—are bankrupt because they fail to recognize the mutual dependence of faith and doubt. Faith without doubt and doubt without faith both lack the necessary depth of the pilgrims' way. Thus, Beckett is closer to true faith than the fundamentalists on either side who settle for cheap certainties.

Jürgen Moltmann exemplified the *theologia viatorum*. In a unique move, he concluded his systematic contributions to theology with a study of his methodology (prolegomena) rather than, what is more typical, beginning with it. He considers theology an "adventure of ideas." The road is not fixed or predetermined. Rather, it "emerged only as I walked it."[98] Because: "It is impossible to say anything that is theologically valid for everyone at all times and in all places."[99] Theology is not a stronghold of eternal truths, with theologians as its gate-keepers. Instead, it is a road, a progression.

We are an exodus people, ever on the way to the promise-land.

Theology must keep this in mind whenever it tries to fix certain truths in place. Theology must learn from its history and the realities of earlier generations, but it must not stay camped out at any one point for too long. We are a mobile people. Our home is God's Kingdom, and it is still to come. Every theology is an anticipation of God's coming, but none are its definitive realization on earth. We await the "unspeakable home" of God's glory. God will write God's own final theology, and everything we produce until then is preliminary. We walk the road of "neither;" we go on, stirring still into the unknown. Faith is a risk and not a certainty. It is a leap in the dark, not a stronghold of unshakability. God is unshakable, and God is certain, but we are human. We are bound to our humanity. Until we are in the fortress of God's new creation and the eternal feast of joy, we remain pilgrims on the way.

4. I CAN'T GO ON, I'LL GO ON

HOPE AND COURAGE

Beckett's famous conclusion to *The Unnamable,* "I can't go on, I'll go on," proclaims a resilient hope rooted in the refusal to accept the world as it is. It is a cry for justice that will not be appeased until all things are made right—until every weeping, lonely maggot is accounted for and comforted. As Karl Ragnar Gierow stated when awarding Beckett the Nobel Prize, "In the realms of annihilation rises the writing of Samuel Beckett like a miserere from all mankind, its muffled minor key sounding liberation to the oppressed, and comfort to those in need."[1] Beckett's resilient hope goes on in the face of utter devastation and despair. His work is permeated with the paradox of such a hope, as David Hesla writes, "In his dark world we can still see a faint glow, a distant point of light, an ember of love, a dim hope."[2] This hope gives a voice to all the hurting and lonely who suffer the pains of this world.

Christian hope, too, is an unnamable, paradoxical hope—it culminates in the radical hope of a future where God will be all in all (1 Cor. 15:28). As Moltmann writes, "Christian hope is a 'hope against hope', or a hope where there is nothing else left to hope for."[3] Believers are often too quick to settle for cheap hopes, the kind of hope we might give ourselves. But the Gospel calls us to look beyond cheap escapism or utopianism and embrace the hope of Christ's cross. Neither naive nor pessimistic, Christian hope is a hope against hope. Beckett's work exemplifies this cadence of hope. When we cannot go on, we go on—not because we find strength in ourselves, but because we are drawn onward by the One who knows our name.

Upon first reading Beckett, it may not be apparent that his work is full of this kind of hope against hope, yet it is one of his most consistent themes. Beckett's world is never totally black; it is never wholly without hope. Because Beckett's work is so systematically unsystematic, iconoclastic, and rooted in cartesian doubt, the appearance of hope is never cheap. It is a costly hope. Hope in Beckett is summed up with the impossible yet inescapable imperative: *on*. Even when his characters curse hope and regret its return, it remains. It is the persistent "perhaps," the going on in spite of everything. As Lawrence Harvey observed, "Hope is badly battered in the rough waters of Beckett's reality, but somehow it never quite goes under."[4] In the bleak landscapes of Beckett's work, the existence of hope is a radical affirmation of defiant humanity in the face of absurdity.

According to Beckett's admission, "perhaps" is the keyword in his plays, as he explained to Tom Driver:

> If life and death did not both present themselves to us, there would be no inscrutability. If there were only darkness, all would be clear. It is because there is not only darkness but also light that our situation becomes inexplicable. Take Augustine's doctrine of grace given and grace withheld: have you pondered the dramatic qualities in this theology? Two thieves are crucified with Christ, one saved and the other damned. How can we make sense of this division? In classical drama, such problems do not arise. [...] But where we have both dark and light we have also the inexplicable. The key word in my plays is 'perhaps.'[5]

This dualism of light and dark is a familiar image in Beckett's work. Indeed, traces of this theme appear in everything he wrote. Richard Kearney dubbed the above statement "Beckett's heart-felt confession of never knowing for certain but always hoping against hope."[6] That is what makes Beckett's world so humane and relatable, but also its supreme challenge. People often read literature to escape into fictional fantasies of comfort, but Beckett refused to allow even fictional certainties. Beckett reveals the world as it is in all its mess and confusion. As such, he is the avowed enemy of fundamentalism, as Kearney goes on to observe: For

Beckett, ideological and religious fanaticism "stems from a denial of the complexities that make up human reality. Beckett's own refusal of easy solutions to life's ultimate questions [...] may well be one of his most abiding gifts."[7] Because there is no simple yes or no, hope is an impossible possibility. It remains in spite of being inexplicable. Beckett's world is neither black nor white but grey.

The theme of impossible hope parallels the theme of protest we discussed in chapter two. It is because we hope—because of the persistent "perhaps"—we remain unreconciled to this world and protest against it. John Calder calls this Beckett's Promethean defiance:

> Above all, despair must be looked at directly and defied. The key word in his work may well be, as he claims, 'perhaps', but the last word he usually leaves us with is 'ON'. When everything else has been removed, one must still strive with a Promethean defiance, as long as human will can function and retain consciousness, to go ON.[8]

The theologian Walter Brueggemann once said that hope is "an absurdity too embarrassing to speak about."[9] Even John Calvin realized that Christian hope is a paradox, writing, "Eternal life is promised to us, but it is promised to the dead."[10] That adds a vital condition to our understanding of hope: we cannot hope in our own strength. Christian hope is an inexplicable absurdity. Resurrection life is promised only to the dead, which means it is a hope against hope. Yet we must go on hoping still.

Christians often think having hope means merely looking on the bright side—as if it is something we can generate in ourselves. But the only real accomplishment of such self-help sentimentalism is the cheapening of hope. Instead, as Brueggemann continues, hope "flies in the face of all those claims we have been told are facts. Hope is the refusal to accept the reading of reality which is the majority opinion."[11] In a sense, the popular sentimental notion of hope is a side-effect of the belief in God as deus ex machina, a concept we rejected in chapter one. God is not the culmination of our best thoughts or ambitions, nor is Christian hope a form of "good vibes" positivity. Our God is the crucified God, and so our hope is a crucified hope. Cheap hope is the hope we give ourselves, but we need an impossible hope, the kind only God provides.

The gift of hope goads us into action for the coming Kingdom, to rebel against this world and refuse to accept it as it is. As Moltmann often stressed, "Through the power of hope, we don't give up, and don't give ourselves up; we remain unreconciled and unaccepting in an unjust and deadly world."[12] We hope, paradoxically, being unable to hope, and despite an unacceptable world. But because this is the world of Christ's cross, it is also a world where hope persists. Herein lies a radical strength to protest against injustice, as Moltmann memorably writes, "Those who hope in Christ can no longer put up with reality as it is, but begin to suffer under it, to contradict it. Peace with God means conflict with the world, for the goad of the promised future stabs inexorably into the flesh of every unfulfilled present."[13] Christian hope is a revolutionary desire for the Kingdom of God.

The persistence of Beckett's hope is a testament to the kind worthy of the Kingdom. Furthermore, his attentiveness to frailty and weakness is a kind of Kingdom-minded devotion, for Christ's Kingdom belongs not to the powerful, confident, rich, or mighty, but to the least of these. Hope as a cheap sentiment does not require justice. In many ways, it perpetuates its opposite by promoting empty escapism over a challenging call to revolution. Indeed, Christian hope demands a better world; it prays and struggles for Kingdom come. Naturally, Beckett does not hope in the Kingdom of God and the new creation of all things, but he nonetheless exemplifies the paradox of hope in his work, as well as hope's struggle for righteousness. For too long, the Church has resigned itself to a cheap hope to match its cheap faith. Beckett's ruthless condemnation of cheap hope can act as a vital corrective against our diseased concept of Christian hope.

In a similar way that Moltmann speaks of hope against hope, Paul Tillich has written movingly about the "courage to be," which he defines as "the courage to accept oneself as accepted in spite of being unacceptable."[14] Courage means going on in spite of the threat of nonbeing, in spite of crushing anxiety and guilt. Such courage "does not remove anxiety," but rather, "takes the anxiety of nonbeing into itself. Courage is self-affirmation 'in spite of,' namely in spite of nonbeing."[15] Thus, Tillich's concept of courage refuses to resign to cheap faith but embraces the reality of nonbeing and doubt. Rather than denying reality as it is, it goes on in spite of its absurdities. In the face of nonbeing, it dares to be. We must courageously confront reality, not escape it. As Tillich writes, "Modern art is not propaganda but revelation. It shows that the reality of our existence is as it is. It does not cover up the reality in which we are living."[16] Along these lines, Beckett's art is extremely courageous. Few writers have embraced brute reality more deeply. His work may be bleak and harsh, but so is the world.

Tillich writes about this tendency in modern art:

> The creators of modern art have been able to see the meaninglessness of our existence; they participate in its despair. At the same time they have the courage to face it and to express it in their pictures and sculptures. They had the courage to be as themselves.[17]

Tillich observes further that "every courage to be has an open or hidden religious root. For religion is the state of being grasped by the power of being-itself."[18] While the religious root may be denied or covered up, it is unavoidable and thus never completely absent in expressions of true hope. Even Beckett thought of poetry as a kind of prayer. Writing to Thomas McGreevy in 1935, he explained, "Yes, prayer rather than poem, in order to be quite clear, because *poems are prayers,* of Dives and Lazarus one flesh."[19] And elsewhere, he writes, "All poetry [...] is prayer."[20] Here Beckett captures well the inescapable humanness of prayer. Prayer is not about begging a cosmic ATM for a hand-out but a human expression of yearning and hope. As Moltmann writes, "Prayer is not something particularly religious; it is something that is profoundly human. It has been said that prayer is the breathing of the soul."[21] Beckett's work is undoubtedly bleak, but its fidelity to an impossible hope makes it a profound testament to human courage. It gives voice to a prayerful lament of an absurd world before the unnamable God. Only when we have given up the God of our own certainties can we embrace the God beyond naming, beyond hope, beyond despair—the God above God. In his courage to be and the paradox of inexplicable hope, Beckett reveals once again how profound his spiritual sensibilities are, contrary to the standard view of crude atheism or empty nihilism. It would be difficult to find a more powerful expression of hope and courage than Beckett's absurd yet persistent imperative: *on.*

The little word "perhaps" that Beckett deemed essential in his work is large enough to express Christian hope and courage. And thus, *perhaps* there is hope for humanity, but it is a crucified hope, a hope on the other side of death. It is hope beyond and against human hope. Whether it is in the despair of crawling through the mud, waiting aimlessly for a relief that never comes, or at the catastrophic endgame of our lives—God is with us in God-forsakenness, ever calling us to go on despite being unable to.

But beyond the hills? Eh? Perhaps it's still green. Eh?

The ending of *The Unnamable* is the most obvious example of this paradoxical hope in Beckett, but we could just as well read the "trilogy" of novels as a prolonged exercise in the removal of false hope and the destruction of false certainties. That goes together with the deconstruction theme we discussed in the previous chapter. What remains at the end is a hope against hope. The process begins with Molloy, who progressively sinks deeper into uncertainty and hopelessness until the almost total loss of identity. It continues with Moran and Malone and the stories of the Unnamable. But beyond the devastation of hopelessness, there remains a radical affirmation: on.

While it would be redundant to look at every example from the trilogy of novels, one stands out as a fascinating illustration. In *Molloy,* Moran reflects on the myth of Sisyphus: "And perhaps he thinks each journey is the first. This would keep hope alive, would it not, hellish hope. Whereas to see yourself doing the same thing endlessly over and over again fills you with satisfaction."[22] This retelling subverts our expectations of the myth. We assume that the Sisyphus' curse is the monotony of daily pushing a boulder up a hill only to watch it roll back to the bottom, but Moran muses that perhaps this repetitive tedium is *a source* of satisfaction he is perpetually denied, not his curse. If Sisyphus were allowed to settle into a familiar routine, then the tortured act of pushing the boulder up the hill would become less horrible day after day. That is the nature of habit. Astutely, this is an apt reflection on human nature and our tendency to prefer habit (the "great deadener") to true freedom. We are often more afraid of freedom than of the bondage of what's familiar because at least habits produce certainty. Freedom is a central component of the uncertainty of our existence. We are never less anxious than when we stand in what Kierkegaard called the "dizziness of freedom." In Moran's retelling, the idea of hope becomes the very mechanism of Sisyphus' torture. Thus, in Moran's version of the myth, his punishment is not the act of rolling the boulder up a hill repeatedly but the illusion that each time is the first, thus denying him the comforts of habit and certainty. It is then fair to say that Sisyphus is tortured by hope as much as, if not more than, the act itself.

Hope is often the agent of torment for Beckett's characters. "Is there then no hope?" asks the voice in *The Unnamable.* To which he replies, "Good gracious, no, heavens, what an idea! Just a faint one perhaps, but which will never serve."[23] Hope is to be feared and rejected, even as a faint glimmer remains inexplicably. Hope is both a terror and mercy. Indeed, in some instances, hope is embraced as a good. In Beckett's most autobiographical piece, *Company,* we read, "Better hope deferred than none. Up to a point. Till the heart starts to sicken."[24] Elsewhere the murmuring voice muses on "light dying" and concludes, "No. No such thing then as no light."[25] Instead, a "faint hope" remains even in hopelessness. The world is not black but grey, so we go on tortured by hope in a seemingly hopeless world. But is it not better to suffer hope than resign to hopelessness? That is the conclusion of Beckett's characters who, while tortured by hope, go on regardless.

Beckett's late *Worstward Ho* also exemplifies this hope against hope with the refrain, "nohow on." The text wrestles with familiar Beckettian themes, such as the inability to express together with the obligation to, and thus, the failure of language. A famous, often-quoted section highlights one of Beckett's central convictions, that *failure* itself is the goal: "All of old. Nothing else ever. Ever tried. Ever failed. No matter. Try again. Fail again. Fail better."[26] The "fail better" motif is not a call to adopt a positive self-help mentality—although that has not stopped the refrain from making its way onto motivational posters and mugs everywhere. Rather, the phrase reflects a tortured admission of failure's inevitability. "Better" is an ironic illusion that torments every lonely maggot bound to the mud. "Better" is the whip at the back of a hope-haunted soul forced to go on without any means of doing so. But courage means to attempt the impossible and fail rather than not to try at all. The tragic irony of this phrase is palpable in the way it has been used by neoliberals to reinforce the banal trivialities of self-helpism amid the failures of late-stage capitalism. (Silicon Valley has practically adopted it as an unofficial mantra.)

Beckett's characters, often themselves authors, strive after the literature of failure. They seek to pierce the veil of hope, but, as John Banville reminds us, "Negation is not nihilism."[27] Nihilism is never the point with Beckett. He strives to unveil the real in the midst of the unreal by relentlessly negating the cheap hopes and nonessential illusions of reality. He strives after a hope beyond cheap comfort, a courageous confrontation with the void that is ever-threatening our lives from day-to-day. In Malone's striving towards death, towards negation, he nonetheless recalls a faint hope familiar to Beckett's world, "For why be discouraged, one of the thieves was saved, that is a generous percentage."[28] The impossibility of ever truly becoming a nihilist is foundational to the realization that even in negation, Beckett's writing is ultimately about a radical hope. Try as his characters might, they can never reach the point of absolute zero; hope remains against all hope.

The Unnamable continues the quest for failure and the fear of hope. In a fascinating passage, the narrator muses:

> I mentioned my hope, but it is not serious. If I could speak and yet say nothing, really nothing? Then I might escape being gnawed to death as by an old satiated rat [...] But it seems impossible to speak and yet say nothing, you think you have succeeded, but you always overlook something, a little yes, a little no, enough to exterminate a regiment of dragoons.[29]

This struggle goes on until the voice says: "I have spoken for my master, listened for the words of my master never spoken, Well done, my child, well done, my son, you may stop, you may go, you are free, you are acquitted, you are pardoned, never spoken."[30] That is an apparent reference to Christ's parable of the talents, especially the pronouncement of the master over his faithful servants, "His lord said unto him, Well done, thou good and faithful servant" (Matthew 25:21, KJV). The voice longs for these words but hears nothing. Thus, the voice lives in the torment of deferred hope, in this case, the hope of rest from striving.

Beckett's protest against cheap hope in these pages is comparable to his protest against God. In *The Unnamable,* the voice quarrels with the curse of his existence, the madness of having nothing to say but having to say it nonetheless. The ultimate source of this absurdity is also the One responsible for the sin of having been born. Like a worm, the voice imagines itself on God's cosmic fishing hook: "The essential is to go on squirming for ever at the end of the line, as long as there are waters and banks and ravening in heaven a sporting God to plague his creature, per pro his chosen shits."[31] But an absurd hope remains: "Stop, perhaps he'll spare me that, have compassion on me and let me stop."[32] In this sense, the name the voice gives itself temporarily, Worm, is an allusion to this image of a ravening (hungry) God fishing the cosmos with a cruel hook. Worm remains on the hook, condemned to a life of squirming on the line. Such bleak imagery reflects Beckett's common refrain about the sin of birth, that to exist is to suffer, and that God is ultimately to blame for each and every injustice.

Yet beyond this God and this hopelessness, there is a crucified Christ and hope against hope. The God that would leave this world in such a cruel state would indeed be the contemptible God of Worm's imagination, and life squirming on the line would be hopeless. The only hope would be to end, to cease to be. Yet, such nihilism is not adopted by Beckett. There remains a glimmer of hope against all hope, even in these brutal images. His writing paradoxically yearns for a hope on the other side of its hopelessness. Just as the iconoclasm of the crucified Christ destroys the idea of an indifferent God who is unmoved by human suffering, so the absurdity of resurrection hope revolts against the cheap hopes we give ourselves; it is a hope beyond hope, hope in the coming of God. The same God who suffered and suffers still with humanity is the God who stands in hopelessness with us awaiting the coming of God. In a sense, this means God awaits God's own redemption just as much as we do. Christ is struggling and suffering on the line with Worm.

Beckett often refuted the charge of nihilism. In conversation with Gottfried Büttner, Beckett lamented, "I simply cannot understand why some people call me a nihilist. There is no basis for that."[33] He cited a line from *Endgame* as an example. Hamm asks: "But beyond the hills? Eh? Perhaps it's still green. Eh? [...] Perhaps you won't need to go very far."[34] Even in one of his bleakest plays, Beckett shows the defiant resilience of hope against hope. Yet, it is also a work that holds out an absurd hope for resurrection. The question remains unanswered. It cannot be. It is a hope against hope, hope on the other side of death. Will Clov leave Hamm and humanity restart? Is there hope for their world? The text ends without answering these questions, just as our lives never receive any certain answer. We go on ever closer to death without any human hope for a beyond—yet on the other side of the cross, there is the resurrection, an absurd hope against hope.

That is precisely the nature of our paradoxical hope. We cannot know what is beyond the door of our lives, what awaits us after our end—if anything or nothing. And this uncertainty infuses us with conflicting despair and hope, a struggle that defines us as humans. Hope against hope embraces the depths of hopelessness yet goes on anyway. Indeed, hope looks like courage in the face of utter darkness and despair. That is the position Beckett places his characters in *Endgame,* and it reflects well the paradox of Christian hope in the resurrection. The game is lost from the start, death is a foregone conclusion, yet we go on nonetheless. Only and always, resurrection is promised to the dead. We are all like Clov, waiting at the door in the bitter uncertainty of what lies beyond. The resurrection hope we profess is thus not a deus ex machina but an absurd hope against hope. We cheapen our hope whenever we pretend it is free from uncertainty, anxiety, and doubt; whenever we turn it into a means of escape rather than a courageous confrontation with brute reality. But as we step through the final door of our lives, we do not go alone—for we profess the name of the One who goes before us and with us, who expects us eagerly and hopes for us. That is our absurd Christian hope.

The Lost Ones

The Lost Ones is a meticulously crafted exploration of a confined, hidden space—of *terra incognita,* hidden earth. Like many of Beckett's late texts, it reads like a film or icon, striving to express images in words. In an enclosed cylinder, several searchers or seekers are described as "lost bodies" that "roam each searching for its lost one."[35] But their cylindrical abode is "Vast enough for search to be in vain."[36] Initially, each lost body's search for their lost one is central, but as the text goes on, it becomes clear that the larger focus is on the search for a way out of the cylinder. The seekers themselves are the lost ones, in that sense. Much of the beauty of the text is in the way Beckett portrays the desperation of their quest. Yet even in its hopelessness, it is not totally without hope.

The text is highly stylistic, even mathematical in its precision. Cohn notes that it took Beckett five years to complete, and even then, his final manuscript listed sixteen problems with the text he could not resolve.[37] Regardless, it is a masterful late work, and one of its central concerns is the dual quest/hope motif. There are also overtones of protest as the lost ones struggle and suffer under the cold indifference of their world.

Two hundred and five lost bodies search tirelessly in a flattened cylinder "fifty metres round and sixteen high" with an omnipresent yellowish light radiating from every side. The image evokes a brutal, inhuman world, a hollow space devoid of recognizable familiarities like dirt or trees or even sky. The fact that it is artificially, inexplicably illuminated only adds to the strangeness. The omnipresent light will sometimes gestate or go dead still, almost as if the cylinder itself were a quasi-divine character. Beckett's paragraphs are dense, the narrator is frequently untrustworthy, and only in the final section does the narrative progress beyond stagnation.

Halfway up the cylinder, there are twenty alcoves or recesses, which the seekers reach with the help of fifteen ladders missing multiple rungs (repurposed as weapons). Only one climber can go on each ladder at a time. The narrator places the cylinder's lost bodies into four categories: the climbers always on the move, the watchers who move and stop, the sedentary ones who remain fixed in place unless stepped on, and the vanquished ones whose heads are lowered in utter paralysis and immobility. But these are not fixed categories, and seekers continually shift between them. At the time of the narration, however, they are mathematically symmetrical, and we can assume this is the kind of problem that Beckett enjoyed solving. There are 5 vanquished, 20 sedentary, 60 watchers, and 120 climbers. Mathematically, there is a kind of beauty to how this might be expressed: (((5 x 4) x 3) x 2). Each parenthetical calculates each category's total, except for the vanquished, which is the first number in the sequence (5). Beckett explains this, in reverse order, "the first are twice as many as the second who are three times as many as the third who are four times as man as the fourth namely five vanquished in all."[38] That is 120, 60, 20, and 5.

Only two of the five vanquished ever receive a description. The narrator indicates that they are the elders of the group, who have already gone through all the other life stages and are now resigned to their condition. The narrator describes one of the vanquished in paragraph ten as a young white-haired woman with a baby in her lap. Then, in paragraph fourteen, a fascinating vanquished one is described as an almost divine woman seated gracefully against the wall with long red hair covering her face and body. She is positioned exactly north in the cylinder and is thus its only fixed orientation. The narrator cryptically states, "She is the north."[39] Therefore, she takes on mythic qualities.

The text also gives the impression that the cylinder is a kind of inferno —which is not surprising when we remember Dante was one of Beckett's favorite writers. The narrator notes, "The effect of this climate on the soul is not to be underestimated."[40] The narrator attempts to describe the lost bodies' activity, and we witness their varied movements from above, but that is also why we get a sense that we cannot trust the narrator. It is an apt comment on all writing and human ideas in general. We are on earth, bound to our cylinder, but we love to pretend we have a privileged place to observe the world objectively from above. We do not, and we suspect the narrator does not either.

A mess of complicated rules and descriptions follows, which becomes uniquely confusing in paragraph twelve. Dominated by mathematically precise movements, life in the cylinder is made to feel illogically legalistic and torturously absurd. The general sense we have from the narrator is that this is a place of intense suffering. The lost bodies suffer from touch but are unable not to touch because of a lack of space. Their skin is extremely dry, presumably due to the light's unrelenting heat, which again echos the inferno symbolism. In contrast, the cylinder itself is impenetrable and rubber-like; it cannot be harmed and retains no indentations or marks. It is, in that sense, like an impassible deity.

The eyes seem to be the only means of communication among the lost ones. That is why the five vanquished close their eyes and are sometimes also called "the blind."[41] Husband and wife couples occasionally exchange a glance in the cylinder before separating again into the mass of lostness. It is clear that love is not what any of them are searching for: "Whatever it is they are searching for it is not that."[42] The eyes seem to be the organ of searching, and the vanquished are not allowed to deny any part of themselves the scrutiny of others. Thus, the story gives off the impression of a maddening, furious search without any hope of success.

The narrator omnisciently prophesies the end of the cylinder, although we hesitate to believe the prediction. Is it false hope? The prophecy is often qualified with "if this notion is maintained," as if the narrator does not even believe it. Indeed, with this phrase, the story ends. However, the prophecy is that one day, when all the searchers have become the vanquished except for one, this last searcher will find the woman with the long red hair, "the north." He will then lift her hair and open her eyes to look at them. Then his own eyes will close as her head falls again. He will move to his final position, which will initiate the end of the cylinder: the temperature will drop to zero, the light will go out, and all will be silent. This prediction seems to offer a strange hope for a way out of the torment, of an end to the endless misery of the quest. Thus, Beckett's story is an imaginative retelling of hell, where the seekers are condemned to search in vain, tortured by the hope of release, yet plagued by the fear that there is no hope. "Abandon all hope ye who enter here." So stated Dante, but those in Beckett's cylinder cannot or will not give up hope. Hope is the very means of their torment.

Two hopes emerge in the narrative. The first is the hope of escape. We hear of this rumor, "From time immemorial rumor has it or better still the notion is abroad that there exists a way out."[43] There are various "schools" of thought that theorize how to find the way out. Some swear by a secret passage through one of the alcoves, while others claim a trapdoor is hidden in the ceiling. But these are not fixed positions. As we learn, "Conversion is frequent."[44] The use of "conversion" is not accidental. Those who profess a way out, an escape, are a clear parody of religions that make similar claims. Even Christianity, which has at its center the crucified Christ, has been too quick to offer cheap escapes rather than courageously confronting life's terrors head-on.

The second hope is the prophetic hope, already mentioned. It is the hope of the vanquished ones, who, it seems, will continue to increase in number as the cylinder progresses. When all have searched exhaustively for escape and resign themselves to hopelessness, the hope is that this will hasten the end of the cylinder itself. It is thus a paradoxical hope: giving up hope is the only hope. The vanquished are apocalyptic in their resignation; their hopelessness is a religious act. But the narrator's uncertainty combined with the ferocity of the searchers ("For the passion to search is such that no place may be left unsearched") makes us question the possibility that seeking will end. Thus, both hopes are presumably false. The seekers will never find a way out, and the vanquished will never convince them to give up trying.

The Lost Ones is a profoundly metaphysical prose poem, a beautiful meditation on seeking, hoping, and despairing in a cruel world. It reflects the human drive to search and understand—even when there is nothing to search for and nothing to know. It thus expresses the human desire to have certainty in uncertainty. Yet this searching and striving for answers will never cease, cannot cease. The narrator's prophecy about the end of seeking is just as unlikely as the end of all human striving. We will never stop hoping, never cease going on, even in the face of complete absurdity and hopelessness. That is clear from one of the text's central lines, "So on infinitely until towards the unthinkable end if this notion is maintained a last body of all by feeble fits and starts is searching still."[45] The end of searching is indeed "unthinkable." At one point in the text, Beckett alludes to the classic image of eternity, often credited to Zeno: "Even so a great heap of sand sheltered from the wind lessened by three grains every second year and every following year increased by two if this notion is maintained."[46] To seek is human. The quest of the lost ones is driven by the absurd hope for a beyond, whether it comes in the form of an escape or end.

The Lost Ones explores how human nature unavoidably creates meaning in meaninglessness and seeks escape where none exists. It succeeds in expressing our deep longing poetically. Some aspects of our nature are indeed better suited to poetic exploration than a dry philosophical treatise. The beauty of Beckett's art is precisely that. If he could express it any other way, he would. But human nature is not so easily defined.

Somewhere in all our mess and confusion, there is an irrevocable longing and hope. Even if we are stripped to our bare essentials, as the characters in Beckett's late work often are, there remains something in us that refuses not to hope. Hope is thus essential to our nature. Yet this longing, this absurd, self-given hope, necessarily points beyond itself to a divine hope, to God's hope. Our hope may be false, but it indicates the possibility that there is a genuine hope beyond finitude. Perhaps our hope is but a type and shadow of the real. The hope we give to ourselves is cheap, but the Christian hope professes a hope beyond human hope. Because it is not grounded in ourselves, it is an unshakable hope. Similar to Beckett's protest atheism against the indifference of God, which nonetheless rests on the basis of seeking after a God above God, so his protest against cheap hope points beyond itself to the yearning for a hope we cannot give ourselves.

The point of Beckett's story, or at least in my reading of it, indicates the impossibility of hopelessness. Even the vanquished, who put on the appearance of resignation, still hope for the end of all striving. In that sense, they are no different than the seekers striving for their "lost one" or for a way out of the cylinder. We might say the pessimists and the optimist both hope for the same end, one by affirmation and the other by negation. Neither are without hope. And thus, hope is an unshakably human predicament. Dante's vision of hell was wrong; it is impossible to abandon all hope. The lost ones will never cease hoping.

Liberated from cheap hope

In 1936, the young Beckett, heavily influenced by Schopenhauer—even going further than him—made this entry in his "Clare Street Notebook:"

> There are moments where the veil of hope is finally ripped away and the eyes, suddenly liberated, see their world as it is, as it must be. Alas, it does not last long, the perception quickly passes: the eyes can only bear such a merciless light for a short while, the thin skin of hope re-forms and one cannot be pierced until it is ripe for decay. Not every cataract ripens: many a human being spends his whole life enveloped in the mist of hope. And even if the cataract can be pierced for a moment it almost always re-forms immediately; and thus it is with hope.[47]

Hope is often a means of unseeing, a distortion of reality. Beckett praises its destruction, but he also recognizes the impossibility of hope's utter demise. That tension is constant in his writing. Hope is a veil that will never be torn. Still, in the act of deconstructing hope, Beckett does not resign to nihilism but embraces the courage of hope amid hopelessness. John Calder once observed, "The more he wallows in the muck the more he extends our idea of beauty."[48] We might augment this apt phrase and say: The more Beckett wallows in hopelessness, the more he extends our idea of hope. Therefore, we should not read Beckett's frequent bouts of hopelessness as the absolute denial of hope but instead as the rejection of all the cheap hopes that keep us bond to illusionary visions of the world. Beckett's unparalleled hopelessness does not reach absolute zero, and therefore, it extends our idea of hope rather than denying it.

Beckett compares piercing the veil of hope to liberation. It is not so much that hope itself is an illusion, but that false hopes keep us bound to the idea of a world we might easily explain. It is this kind of escapist hope that Beckett rejects. Yet in rejecting it, he embraces a larger hope, a hope beyond illusions. As Jack MacGowran movingly observed, "He's written about human distress not human despair. Everything in his work ends with hope. Hope, hope, in everything he writes. I've never met a man with so much compassion for the human race."[49] This reading is drastically different from the common caricatures of Beckett. But as I have tried to show, it is the best way to understand him.

In plunging the depths of human misery and hopelessness, Beckett pays homage to the resilience of human hope. He displays unique compassion by refusing all false comforts and cheap solutions and instead embracing uncertainty. In this, we discover a forceful and profound affirmation of hope. The courage to go on when we cannot is the foundation of Beckett's radical hope against hope.

Martin Esslin once described Beckett as

> [A] lone figure, without hope of comfort, facing the great emptiness of space and time without the possibility of miraculous rescue or salvation, in dignity, resolved to fulfill its obligation to express its own predicament [...] And if it is the living, existential experience of the individual that matters and has precedence over any abstract concepts it may elicit, then the very act of confronting the void, or continuing to confront it, *is an act of affirmation.*[50]

It is in this sense that Beckett's writing is fundamentally courageous and life-affirming. It confronts the horrors of human history without succumbing to the cheap hopes and answers that many so often default to. In Beckett's work, as in life, there are no ways out, no bargain truths that will make any sense of this mess. Indeed, there is nothing to express and no means to express, yet we must express because not to would mean giving up, resigning to nothingness, and ceasing to be human. Beckett performs one of literature's most concrete acts of affirmation with his paradoxical hope and courageous confrontation with life. He does not affirm a world that does not exist, the world as we imagine it, but the world as it is, in all its absurdity and sorrow. And that is what makes his work so beautiful.

Alan Schneider summarizes well the comforting endurance of Beckett's hope:

> His words strike to the very marrow—the sudden sharp anguish of a Pozzo or of a Hamm crying out for understanding in an uncertain universe; Clov's detailed description of the bleak harsh landscape of our existence on earth. While against and in spite of the harshness and the uncertainty, there is the constant assertion of man's will, and spirit, his sense of humor, as the only bulwarks against despair; the constant 'glimmers of hope', even in the dark depths of that abyss in which we find ourselves.[51]

In a roundabout way, Beckett's hope echoes the theological insights of Jürgen Moltmann regarding the nature of Christian hope as a hope against hope. Moltmann writes, "When we look towards the open future, dark and undetermined as it is, it is hope that gives us courage."[52] Genuine hope means facing reality with resilience, not resignation. Christian hope does not turn a blind eye to the plight of the oppressed. Indeed, the hope we have in God's coming Kingdom is not other-worldly. As much as escapism has infected the Church, the Gospel is not about going to heaven when we die but of ushering in God's Kingdom "on earth as it is in heaven." That is why Moltmann consistently linked the hope we have for God's coming with the strength to resist injustice. In anticipation of the new creation of all things, we fight with the assurance that righteousness and justice will prevail. It is an absurd hope, but we go on nonetheless. As Moltmann often noted, hope is a command. Thus, much like Beckett's literary dilemma to express without being able to express, we are commanded to hope, being unable to hope without God's hope.

False hope comforts the privileged like blinders over their eyes, guarding their illusions against remembering the plight of the least of these. Thus, false hope is more dangerous to the Christian faith than doubt or despair. By numbing us from the brute realities of life, it is the sand in which we bury our heads to quiet the screams of hopelessness in our world. And ultimately, false hope denies the power of Christ's cross by turning it into a cheap religious symbol. But the cross is not confined to an altar. The cross is with the incarcerated, homeless, hungry, poor, and sick. If ever we turn a blind eye to the least of these, we forsake the cross of Christ. Indeed, Christ is still being crucified among us.[53] He is with every victim of injustice. But even hell is not without hope because Christ descended into hell.

James Cone also recognized the connection between suffering and courage, writing, "Faith in Christ therefore does not explain evil; it empowers us to fight against evil. […] Evil remains inexplicable, not in spite of faith but because of it."[54] Genuine hope does not make excuses for evil, nor does it turn a blind eye to suffering. Rather, hope and faith in God gives us the courage to confront atrocities and fight to overcome them in Christ's name. Hope is never passive.

Christians may read Beckett's despair and hopelessness as an offense against the Gospel, yet that is precisely the problem with shallow Christianity. If our hope is so fragile that despair, hopelessness, and God-abandonment can threaten to destroy it entirely, then it is not the same hope the Gospel proclaims. It is not the hope that arises from God-forsakenness and death, but the kind of cheap sentimental hope we give ourselves, hope in positivity and progress. The Christian hope begins with the hopelessness of the cross, and therefore, it is large enough and strong enough to include all darkness, suffering, and despair. Like Bonhoeffer's cheap grace, cheap hope is the hope we give to ourselves, but it is shallow and selfish. We need the kind of hope that we cannot give ourselves, hope beyond our wildest imagination. God hopes for us and waits for us. God's hope is the foundation of our Christian hope.

God's future and hope

God's hope is not often a subject of Christian theology. It is more common to imagine God as a cosmic puppet master determining the end of history. But Moltmann challenges this faulty notion. Rather than speculatively assuming God's future is closed and predetermined, Moltmann argues for an open future even for God. God is not already in glory without us but anticipates the future glorification of all things. Thus, hope is not just a human phenomenon. If God's future is fixed, there is nothing for God to hope for, but instead, only to accept fate and wait patiently;

but if God's future is open, then God hopes and struggles for the future together with humanity. Moltmann derives this concept from the *kenosis* of God, God's self-emptying love revealed in the cross. God limits Godself for the sake of giving space for creation to flourish. That means Christian hope can and must be rooted in God's hope, in the realization that God hopes together with us for the new creation of all things. "So, instead of maintaining that God must know and predict everything," writes Moltmann, "we now say that the living God does not know everything in advance, because God has no wish to do so. [...] God's providence is directed not to future realities but to future possibilities."[55] The future is open, and thus, we may speak of God's expectant hope for a new world yet to come.

For Moltmann, Christian hope looks like unrest spurred on by attentive anticipation. Hope enlivens our senses to see the way things could be, that a better world is possible. Hope includes the realization that, as David Graeber writes, "The ultimate, hidden truth of the world is that it is something that we make, and could just as easily make differently."[56] Thus, hope thrusts us into conflict with the world and its tragedies. The enemy of hope is apathy, not hopelessness. Because even in hopelessness, there is a struggle, but apathy is the victory of paralysis, the loss of taste and sense for the new and possible. We should never be so indifferent to suffering that we are no longer disturbed by the injustices of our world. God, too, is discontent with the world as it is, and together with humanity, God eagerly anticipates "the fullness of God and the feast of eternal joy."[57] God hopes and waits for the day when God will be "all in all," when all will be made new. God hopes for the cosmic Easter, the new creation of all things.

Something drastic happens to our perception of the world when we realize history is not a series of predetermined events. That we can change things, and nothing is fixed. To wait for the Kingdom does not mean doing nothing but to anticipate and struggle for the future. We often use our concept of God's almightiness as an excuse to accept the world as it is, to leave it unchallenged and unquestioned. Christians have justified numerous atrocities throughout history accordingly. Slaveholders taught African slaves a Gospel that denied any concept of liberty on earth in favor of a spiritual escape in heaven. Today, many in the Church accept a Gospel that does not confront the systems of oppression in this world but resigns itself to merely "saving souls" without liberating captives, proclaiming good news to the poor, or sight to the blind, as Christ proclaimed (Luke 4:18).

In the darkness of the present, God waits with us for the redemption of all creation. But God's waiting is not passive; it is active anticipation of the coming Kingdom. In my reading of Beckett's great play of waiting and hope, *Waiting for Godot,* I theologically placed God amid the absurdity of their waiting. God is not the absent Godot character. God is with Didi and Gogo, Pozzo and Lucky, as they tragically and comically wait without certainty for salvation. As one critic remarked, the play is "a threnody [lament] of hope deceived and deferred but never extinguished; a play suffused with tenderness for the whole human perplexity."[58] Likewise, the message of the resurrection is proclaimed to those who must die. In our finite hopelessness, God comes to us and suffers with us to hope with us, to proclaim a beyond. But God's hope is never passive; it includes God's relentless struggle for justice. Wherever liberation is on the move, God is working. To be the hands and feet of God, we must be agents of revolutionary change in this world. As Dorothee Soelle powerfully saw, "God has no other hands than ours."[59] In solidarity with all those who suffer, God hopes with a "hope deceived and deferred but never extinguished," and God waits and fights in expectant hope for God's future and ours.

We have identified Christ's presence in the character's suffering, but we must also identify God's eschatological hope in their waiting. While it is true, theologically, that God goes ahead of us in the resurrection life of Christ, it is also true that God has so bound God's fate with the fate of humanity that God remains unreconciled to the future until all things are made new. *God waits for us.* God so loves and delights in the human race as to bind God's fate to ours. But God also waits *with us,* patiently suffering the unredeemed present for the sake of the future world that is to come. As Moltmann writes, "God isn't silent. God isn't dead. God is waiting."[60] It is our great comfort to know that we do not wait alone, that there is someone on the other side of our struggles for justice, as Moltmann writes movingly:

> God is for me; I am his child. Christ is beside me; I am his brother. Whether this makes me believe more strongly or whether I doubt all the

> more, whether I am swallowed up in the darkness of night or find myself at the dawn of a new day—I know: there is someone waiting for me, who will not give me up, who goes ahead of me, who lifts me up, someone to whom I am important.[61]

The distinction between the hope we give ourselves and God's hope for the future is exemplified well in Moltmann's theological affirmation of universalism. When considering the question of the restoration of all things, Moltmann reflected, "If I examine myself seriously, I find that I have to say: I myself am not a universalist, but God may be one."[62] This difference is crucial. It involves the refusal to base hope on ourselves. Instead, we rely on God's hope for the future as the source of our hope. When we consider our limited hope, we come up short. But God's hope is more extravagant, and, as Moltmann later concludes, it is a hope big enough for the redemption of all creation. Thus, for God's sake, we affirm the restoration of all things: "Universalism is not the substance of the Christian proclamation; it is its presupposition and its goal. 'Behold, I make all things new': if that really is God's future, then everyone is invited and no one is shut out."[63] The question of universalism involves the fate of humanity and our ultimate hope for justice and mercy, that God will make all things right. Thus, it is, above all else, God's question. God will not be true to Godself unless all is made right and mercy and justice meet. If even one person is eternally lost or one maggot is forsaken, then God ceases to be our God, God-for-us. If suffering, oppression, and the "open wound" of history are not accounted for and rectified, God is not the God of love and justice. The very God-ness of God is at stake.

Even if we are swallowed up in the darkness and despair of life, we are nonetheless hoped for and expected. We have a hope that is not rooted in our capacities but founded on the hope of God, the waiting of God, and the joy of God's expectation. Christ waits for Godot with us. It is a certain hope, yet one beyond the cheap certainties we prefer. It is a hope against hope.

I can't go on, I'll go on. I can't go on because this world is dark, unjust, and full of absurd tragedies. I possess in myself little capacity for hope. But I go on anyway, hoping against hope because God's Spirit dwells in me and comforts me. "In the *pathos* of God," explains Moltmann, "man is filled with the spirit of God. [...] He is angry with God's wrath. He suffers with God's suffering. He loves with God's love. He hopes with God's hope."[64] God's capacity for hope is the source of our hope. I go on because God has gone before me, expects me, and prepares a way for me. Even if I am lost to darkness and despair, even if I am hopeless, even if I am dead, Christ waits for me and hopes for me. That is the proper form of Christian hope, in the end. It is a hope given only to the dead. Thus, no matter what I do or fail to do, God is my beyond. It is a hope against hope, firmly built on the foundation of Jesus Christ, crucified and risen.

CONCLUSION

Samuel Beckett expresses, with an unparalleled depth of feeling and beauty, the experience of human suffering, protest, longing, and hope. His work has made an irrevocable difference to my existence. Few Christians would be willing to consider Beckett a source of spiritual comfort and theological iconoclasm. But throughout this study, I hope to have shown that no such contradiction needs exist. It is only the false discord of a shallow faith and a poor reading of Beckett that considers the two to be enemies. They can, and perhaps must, be seen as standing on common ground. I have no illusions of synthesizing them into one consistent vision, but the Christian faith shares more with Beckett than we have often been willing to concede.

I do not share Beckett's hesitation to confess the creeds of our faith. However, I do sympathize with his unrelenting doubt in all inadequate, human-made systems. I share his fears about death and cannot easily shake the brute reality of my mortality. I believe and hope in the resurrection life yet to come and trust that life will triumph over death, but it is a costly hope. Beckett's rejection of cheap faith has helped strengthen my faith in God rather than diminish it. He has laid bare the uncertainties of existence, but that has only led to a deeper sense of awe before its endless mysteries. He has cured any sense of cheap faith in me. Cheap faith longs for easy believism and pat answers to difficult questions, but the Christian confession is not about having all the answers to life's mysteries, nor is it always an easy source of comfort. Faith plunders the depths of the human condition and makes no bones about being easy or safe. In the memorable phrase of C. S. Lewis, Aslan is not safe, but he's good. The quest of faith is neither safe nor free from doubt; it is an uncertain road, but it is good and right and beautiful. Beckett walked that uncertain road courageously.

If faith is the same as certainty, then Beckett was faithless. And so am I. But if faith is, instead, a kind of courage in the face of uncertainty, then Beckett was a man of tremendous faith. In fact, if the God we Christians confess is the same God that Beckett protests against with such bitter and blasphemous words, then I am no Christian either. But there is a God beyond the gods we fashion for ourselves, a God above God, the kind of God who does the unthinkable and ungodly thing of becoming a man to suffer and die and proclaim an extravagant word of hope to the darkest depths of hell. That is precisely the God I confess, and Beckett's relentless iconoclasm against all false gods is a vital reminder of the commandment against idolatry. As John Calvin wrote, "The human heart is a factory of idols."[1] So we must be vigilant and perpetual skeptics ready to demolish all human-made gods.

In a moral sense, Beckett has also taught me what it means to see the "least of these" in the everyday down-and-outs of society. His characters are the poor and lowly, the unwell and powerless outcasts. Beckett writes one of the most compassionate portraits of human nature I have ever read by centering his vision on the plight of the weak and forgotten. Theologically speaking, he re-presents Christ in the least of these so that we can see the presence of God not merely in the high and mighty but chiefly and firstly in the poor and oppressed. If we cannot read Beckett's broken, despairing characters and see Christ in their midst, then perhaps we cannot see Christ at all.

Artistically, few writers were more courageous in their quest for experimentation than Beckett. His work is exceedingly beautiful, thoughtful, and innovative. His depth of feeling, mastery of language, and creative genius make him the Shakespeare of our era—though perhaps exceedingly more relevant and beautiful.

As a writer, no one has taught me more about the creative process and what it means to write. I keep on my desk a rotating selection of advice from his letters. For example, this important reminder: "Work, work, writing for nothing and yourself, don't make the silly mistake we all make of publishing too soon."[2] I often think of this, especially the need to work for nothing and no one but the work itself. Beckett's courage to confront the white page and risk the "siege in the room" is what inspires me so much as a writer. He once explained to Lawrence Harvey, "I write because I have to. What do you do when 'I can't' meets 'I must'?"[3] All of his writing is, in a sense, about the struggle of a writer with their writing. And in that struggle, he touches upon something profoundly human. He provides a vulnerable examination of the doubts and fears which plague every artist. I felt a strange kinship with Beckett when I read about how, after winning the Nobel Prize, he wrote to a friend that perhaps his career was no more than one long "blunder," and then wondered if life would have been better if he had gone to work for Guinness as his father wanted.[4] He writes about writing and the obligation to be a writer despite being unable to write adequately. And this inspires radical courage. "I can't go on, I'll go on" is not merely a mantra for life but also writing. When I cannot write, I write.

Life is a struggle. But it is also a great joy. As much as Beckett's work affirms life in an oddly paradoxical sense, as a Christian, I feel it is important to be more direct in the affirmation of life. As Moltmann reminds us, "Human life has to be affirmed [...] The affirmation of life that is inherent in God's love is greater than the denial of life from which we suffer."[5] That touches upon the duality of existence. We cannot have life on any other terms than its totality, joy and suffering together. As Beckett never ceased to stress, it is because there is both light and dark that all is inexplicable. But we must find the courage to say Yes to life in spite of the darkness, to go on when we cannot. Beckett's emphasis on the darkness and absurdity of life is necessary, but it is also incomplete without the confession of hope, that the love of God overcomes the darkness. This hope is the unnamable something that gives us the strength to go on and on with our wounds.

I have a firm hope in the world that is to come, in the Kingdom Christ proclaimed. But my hope does not resolve the struggle of doubt and uncertainty. Beckett's work cures our obsession with cheap hope, and therefore, it is a reminder of the hope that only God can provide. Resurrection hope is a hope on the other side of death, an absurd hope against hope. We cannot hope, but we go on hoping. Or, in the words of scripture, "I believe; help my unbelief" (Mark 9:24, NKJV).

As much as we would like to ignore human distress and pretend life is one endless parade of bliss, it is not, and we cannot. We cannot shut our ears or close our eyes to the cries of the poor and the oppressed all around us because these are the cries of Christ. We wait for Godot, yearn with an eager expectation for the redemption of this world. Beckett's work is so universal because suffering and distress are so human. All of us, together with creation, groan and long for justice and mercy. To read Beckett is to be reminded of this groaning, not to shut our ears to it, but to join the cosmic protest. Moltmann and other theologians like him who have embraced the theology of God's co-suffering love—all those who profess that God suffers *with* humanity rather than standing above us as an impassible observer—have seen that this leads, necessarily, to moral and political action in this world. We refuse to accept the world as it is and strive to change it in hopeful anticipation of the coming Kingdom. We must hear Christ in the cries of the oppressed. That means opening our eyes and ears to see and hear the least of these. As Moltmann writes, "To go open-eyed through life, to recognize Christ in unnoticeable people, in presence of mind to do the right thing at the right time—that is what praying and watching is about. We believe in order to see, and to affirm what we see."[6]

Through the great depths of his compassion and literary solidarity with the suffering poor and oppressed, his relentless protest against injustice and God-forsakenness, his quest for meaning and the unnamable Other, and his hope against hope, Samuel Beckett is among the most courageous writers of our age. Few have wrestled as beautifully with the big questions of our existence, the silent cries of our souls, and the longing for God at the center of our God-forsaken spaces. His paradoxical spirituality is among the most profound I've encountered. He is complex and challenging, but he is also extremely simple. He reaches the pit of our shared humanity and touches a nerve in us all. As it was astutely observed to Jack MacGowran by a young teenager: "The more I read Sam Beckett and feel his compassion for the human condition, I realize that the magnitude of my own youthful and harrowing problems need no longer be a tortured secret, but can really be understood and shared, and my existence made much more tolerable."[7]

"You're on Earth," Hamm lamented, "there's no cure for that."[8] But we are not alone, and this is our great comfort, our absurd hope. We have a brother in suffering, a friend in hopelessness. We have a God who shares our grief, a God whose future is on the way, whose love has conquered death, who here and now invites us to anticipate the feast of eternal joy in the new creation of God's delight. Beckett's art is spiritual poetry, a mystical icon of suffering, protest, quest, and hope. There is much we can learn from his courageous words.

NOTES

Introduction

1. *The Theology of Samuel Beckett,* 13. London: Calder Publications, 2012.
2. Ibid., 108.
3. Fundamentalism is often rooted in an understanding of the Bible that rigidly assumes its infallibility, as Jürgen Moltmann writes: "Fundamentalism fossilizes the Bible into an unquestionable authority." *The Crucified God,* 8. Minneapolis, MN: Fortress Press, 1993.
4. *Samuel Beckett: Anatomy of a Literary Revolution,* "Introduction" by Eagleton, 2. New York: Verso Books, 2006.
5. *The Selected Works of Samuel Beckett,* IV, 495. New York: Grove Press, 2010. Hereafter abbreviated "SBW."
6. Eberhard Jüngel: "Pauline theology as a whole is a theology of the cross and nothing else." *Death: The Riddle and the Mystery,* 97. Philadelphia: The Westminster Press, 1974.
7. *Journals of Søren Kierkegaard,* Nov. 20, 1847.
8. *The Letters of Samuel Beckett: 1929-1940,* 520. Cambridge: Cambridge University Press, 2009.
9. SBW I, 373.
10. *Samuel Beckett: The Last Modernist,* 359. New York: HarperCollins, 1996.
11. *Beckett: A Guide for the Perplexed,* 24. New York: Continuum International Publishing Group, 2008.
12. SBW IV, 563.
13. Ibid., 556.
14. SBW IV, 425.
15. *Beckett Remembering Remembering Beckett,* 47. New York: Arcade Publishing, 2014.
16. *Damned to Fame,* 439. New York: Simon & Schuster, 1996.
17. *Silence,* 51. Middletown, CT: Wesleyan University Press, 1961. Beckett actually echoes this phrase, or is perhaps its origin, saying to Robert Blin: "I have nothing to say but I can only say to what extent I have nothing to say." Cited in John Pilling: *Samuel Beckett,* 22. London: Routledge & Kegan Paul Ltd, 1976.
18. Trans. by Ruby Cohn: *Samuel Beckett: The Comic Gamut,* 166. New Brunswick, NJ: Rutgers University Press, 1962.
19. SBW IV, 316.
20. Ibid., 556.
21. *Samuel Beckett: A Critical Heritage,* 240. London: Routledge & Kegan Paul Ltd, 1979.
22. *Samuel Beckett: Poet & Critic,* 373. Princeton: Princeton University Press, 1970.
23. *Samuel Beckett: A Critical Heritage,* 217. London: Routledge & Kegan Paul Ltd,

1979. On this, Ruby Cohn writes: "I think he meant this literally. After absorbing so much knowledge, Beckett became aware that one can know too much to know, that one must return to the innocence of stupidity in order to feel." *Back to Beckett*, 119. Princeton University Press, 1973.

24. SBW IV, 492.

1. He Leaves No Maggot Lonely

1. *Samuel Beckett: The Critical Heritage,* 220. London: Routledge & Kegan Paul Lt, 1979.
2. *Beckett at 60,* 82. London: Calder and Boyars Ltd, 1967.
3. *The Letters of Samuel Beckett: 1957-1965,* 582. Cambridge: Cambridge University Press, 2014.
4. *Samuel Beckett: The Critical Heritage,* 217. London: Routledge & Kegan Paul Ltd, 1979.
5. Ibid., 217.
6. *The Shape of Paradox,* 44. Los Angeles: University of California Press, 1978.
7. *Letters and Papers from Prison,* 479. DBW Vol. 8. Minneapolis, MN: Fortress Press, 2010.
8. SBW III, 61.
9. SBW II, 59.
10. *Back to Beckett,* 128. Princeton: Princeton University Press, 1973.
11. *Casebook on Waiting for Godot,* 83. Ed. Ruby Cohn. New York: Grove Press, 1967.
12. *Damned to Fame*, 369. New York: Simon & Schuster, 1996.
13. Ibid., 566.
14. SBW III, 21.
15. SBW III, 27.
16. SBW III, 67.
17. SBW III, 68.
18. SBW III, 70.
19. Scripture quotations here and throughout (unless otherwise noted) are from New Revised Standard Version Bible: Anglicized Edition, copyright © 1989, 1995 National Council of the Churches of Christ in the United States of America. Used by permission. All rights reserved worldwide.
20. SBW III, 75.
21. SBW III, 80.
22. SBW III, 81.
23. *The Crucified God*, 24. Minneapolis, MN: Fortress Press, 1993.
24. SBW III, 5.
25. SBW III, 45.
26. SWB III, 52.
27. SBW III, 67.
28. SBW III, 67.
29. SBW III, 83.
30. SBW III, 84.
31. *Beckett at 60,* 86. London: Calder and Boyars Ltd, 1967.
32. Moltmann writes: "[T]he cross is the really irreligious thing in Christian faith. It is the suffering of God in Christ, rejected and killed in the absence of God, which qual-

ifies Christian faith as faith, and as something different from the projection of man's desire." *The Crucified God,* 37. Minneapolis, MN: Fortress Press, 1993.

33. Qohelet 1:1, Robert Alter trans., *The Hebrew Bible.* New York: W. W. Norton & Company, 2019.
34. Aug. 31, 2016: https://www.youtube.com/watch?v=4HHR_3HJdEQ; 3:10-3:19. Italics mine.
35. *Experiences in Theology,* 305. Minneapolis, MN: Fortress Press, 2000.
36. *Church Dogmatics* IV/1, 186. New York; London: T&T Clark, 2004.
37. *God's Being Is in Becoming,* 99. Grand Rapids, MI: Wm. B. Eerdmans Publishing Co., 2001.
38. *The Trinity and the Kingdom,* 49. Minneapolis, MN: Fortress Press, 1993.
39. Eberhard Jüngel: "This God loves man and it is for this reason that he suffers for man. Man's suffering is finite. God, however, is not the kind of God who does not suffer at all. He is the God who has a capacity for *infinite* suffering, and it is because of his love that he suffers infinitely. *This* is why he is death's conqueror." *Death: The Riddle and the Mystery,* 112. Philadelphia: The Westminster Press, 1974.
40. *The Crucified God,* 205. Minneapolis, MN: Fortress Press, 1993.
41. Moltmann's theodicy is more complex than these brief reflections seem to imply. His work *God in Creation,* for example, establishes a highly original approach to the question of evil. See also his important book, *The Trinity and the Kingdom.*
42. SBW III, 90.
43. SBW III, 139.
44. SBW III, 122.
45. SBW III, 123.
46. SBW III, 124.
47. See SBW III, 98.
48. SBW III, 139.
49. SBW III, 127-8.
50. SBW III, 139.
51. SBW III, 144.
52. SBW III, 130.
53. *Damned to Fame,* 402. New York: Simon & Schuster, 1996.
54. *The Crucified God,* 249. Minneapolis, MN: Fortress Press, 1993.
55. SBW III, 134.
56. SBW III, 102.
57. *Samuel Beckett: The Critical Heritage,* 223. London: Routledge & Kegan Paul Ltd, 1979.
58. *A Beckett Canon,* 45. Ann Arbor: The University of Michigan Press, 2001.
59. See ibid., 45-47.
60. SBW IV, 88.
61. SBW IV, 87.
62. SBW IV, 86.
63. *The Hebrew Bible,* Robert Alter trans. New York: W. W. Norton & Company, 2019.
64. SBW IV, 35.
65. *Samuel Beckett: Poet & Critic,* 156. Princeton: Princeton University Press, 1970.
66. SBW III, 449.
67. SBW III, 80.
68. SBW IV, 492.
69. SBW VI, 298.
70. *In the End—The Beginning,* 84-5. Minneapolis, MN: Fortress Press, 2004.

71. *Samuel Beckett: The Critical Heritage,* 219. London: Routledge & Kegan Paul Ltd, 1979.
72. *Beckett Remembering Remembering Beckett,* 202. New York: Arcade Publishing, 2014.
73. Ibid.
74. Ibid., 282.
75. Ibid., 151.
76. *The Crucified God,* 46-7. Minneapolis, MN: Fortress Press, 1993.
77. *Letters and Papers from Prison,* 479. DBW Vol. 8. Minneapolis, MN: Fortress Press, 2010.
78. *Night,* 64. New York: Hill & Wang, 2006.
79. *The Crucified God,* 274. Minneapolis, MN: Fortress Press, 1993.
80. SBW III, 81.
81. *Samuel Beckett: The Critical Heritage,* 221. London: Routledge & Kegan Paul Ltd, 1979.

2. She Rails at the Source of All Life

1. Deirdre Bair: *Samuel Beckett,* 528. New York: Simon & Schuster, 1993.
2. Ibid.
3. *Samuel Beckett,* 117. London: Routledge & Kegan Paul Ltd, 1976.
4. *Experiences in Theology,* 16. Minneapolis, MN: Fortress Press, 2000.
5. *The Crucified God,* 226-7. Minneapolis, MN: Fortress Press, 1993.
6. *A Broad Place,* 79. Minneapolis, MN: Fortress Press, 2009.
7. *Ecumenical, Academic, and Pastoral Work: 1931-1932,* 260. DBW Vol. 11. Minneapolis, MN: Fortress Press, 2012.
8. *A Broad Place,* 151. Minneapolis, MN: Fortress Press, 2009.
9. *Iconic Spaces,* 6. Notre Damne: The University of Notre Dame Press, 2007.
10. *Samuel Beckett,* 93. New York: Grove Press, 1968.
11. SBW I, 295; italics mine.
12. SBW III, 104.
13. SBW III, 105.
14. *Samuel Beckett: The Last Modernist,* 557. New York: HarperCollins Publishers, 1996.
15. *The Crucified God,* 221. Minneapolis, MN: Fortress Press, 1993.
16. *Beckett at 60,* 43. London: Calder and Boyars, 1967.
17. *God, the Quest, the Hero,* 265. Chapel Hill, NC: University of North Carolina Press, 1988.
18. *Samuel Beckett,* 119. London: Routledge & Kegan Paul Ltd, 1976.
19. SBW II, 37.
20. *The Hebrew Bible,* Robert Alter trans. New York: W. W. Norton & Company, 2019.
21. SBW III, 127.
22. SBW II, 411.
23. Ibid.
24. Ibid., 412.
25. Ibid., 414.
26. *God, the Quest, the Hero,* 259. Chapel Hill, NC: University of North Carolina Press, 1988.
27. SBW II, 418.
28. Ibid.

29. Anthony Cronin reprints the photo in his biography of Beckett: *Samuel Beckett: The Last Modernist,* 310. New York: HarperCollins Publishers, 1997.
30. SBW II, 434.
31. Ibid., 438.
32. Ibid., 442.
33. Ibid., 444.
34. Ibid.
35. Ibid., 452.
36. Ibid., 460
37. Ibid, 463.
38. Ibid.
39. SBW II, 466.
40. Ibid., 468.
41. Qohelet 1:1. *The Hebrew Bible,* Robert Alter trans. New York: W. W. Norton & Company, 2019.
42. SBW II, 476.
43. Ibid., 480.
44. Ibid., 482.
45. Ibid., 486.
46. Ibid., 493.
47. Ibid., 504.
48. SBW II, 510.
49. Ibid., 514.
50. Ibid., 516.
51. Ibid., 520
52. Ibid.
53. Ibid.
54. SBW IV, 378.
55. SBW II, 247.
56. M. Gusson, 'Beckett Distills his Vision' in The New York Times, (31 July 1983), section H, p 3.
57. SBW IV, 451.
58. *Damned to Fame*, 588. New York: Simon & Schuster, 1996.
59. SBW IV, 451.
60. Adopted from Marjorie Perloff's essay, *On Beckett,* 191; ed. S. E. Gontarski. New York: Grove Press, 1986.
61. *A Beckett Canon,* 363. Ann Arbor, MI: The University of Michigan Press, 2001.
62. SBW IV, 462.
63. SBW IV, 469.
64. SBW IV, 455.
65. SBW IV, 468.
66. *Samuel Beckett: Playwright & Poet,* 129. Ed. by Christopher Murray. New York: Pegasus Books, 2009.
67. SBW IV, 470.
68. *Iconic Spaces: The Dark Theology of Samuel Beckett's Drama.* Wynands does not explicitly discuss *Ill Seen Ill Said,* but here overall point applies well to the text.
69. SBW IV, 460.
70. SBW IV, 325.
71. SBW II, 227.
72. Barge, "The Empty Heaven of Samuel Beckett," 17.

73. *The Trinity and the Kingdom,* 48. Minneapolis, MN: Fortress Press, 1993.
74. *The Hidden Question of God,* 10. Grand Rapids, MI: Wm. B Eerdmans Publishing Company, 1977.
75. Ibid., 144.
76. See Amiran's interesting literary and biographical comparison of Augustine and Beckett: *Wandering and Home,* 144-6. University Park, PA: The Pennsylvania State University Press, 1993.
77. *The Crucified God,* 246. Minneapolis, MN: Fortress Press, 1993.
78. Moltmann writes: "The symbol of the cross in the church points to the God who was crucified not between two candles on an altar, but between two thieves in the place of the skull, where the outcasts belong, outside the gates of the city. It does not invite thought but a change of mind. It is a symbol which therefore leads out of the church and out of religious longing into the fellowship of the oppressed and abandoned." Ibid., 40.

3. Unspeakable Home

1. *Iconic Spaces,* 18. Notre Dame, IN: University of Notre Dame Press, 2007.
2. Ibid., 5.
3. *On the Trinity,* 3.24 and 2.7. Public domain.
4. *Iconic Spaces,* 46. Notre Dame, IN: University of Notre Dame Press, 2007.
5. *Dynamics of Faith,* 44-5. New York: Harper & Row, 1957.
6. *The Word of God and the Word of Man,* 186. Grand Rapids, MI: Zondervan Publishing House, 1935.
7. SBW IV, 556.
8. Ibid., 563.
9. *The Letters of Samuel Beckett: 1929-1940,* 518. Cambridge: Cambridge University Press, 2009.
10. Ibid.
11. *Iconic Spaces,* 44. Notre Dame, IN: University of Notre Dame Press, 2007.
12. Ibid., 185.
13. SBW IV, 57.
14. *Ulysses,* 34.
15. SBW IV, 60.
16. SBW IV, 58.
17. SBW IV, 60.
18. Combs, Eugene: "Impotence and Ignorance: A Parody of Prerogatives in Samuel Beckett," *Studies in Religion/Sciences Religieuses,* 2 (1972), 125.
19. Ibid.
20. Jaroslav Pelikan: *The Spirit of Eastern Christendom (600-1700): The Christian Tradition Vol. 2,* 258. Chicago: The University of Chicago Press, 1974.
21. *The Theology of Samuel Beckett,* 124. London: Calder Publications, 2012.
22. *Iconic Spaces,* 48. Notre Dame, IN: University of Notre Dame Press, 2007.
23. *Experiences in Theology,* 173. Minneapolis, MN: Fortress Press, 2000.
24. Ibid.
25. *Samuel Beckett's Novel* Watt, 124. Philadelphia: University of Pennsylvania Press, 1984.
26. *The Long Sonata of the Dead,* 30. New York: Grove Press, 1969.
27. SBW I, 197.

28. SBW I, 199.
29. *The Letters of Samuel Beckett: 1957-1965,* 82. Cambridge: Cambridge University Press, 2014.
30. Ibid.
31. SBW I, 203-4.
32. X.6, 8. Moltmann responded to this prayer with his own mysticism of the body, which is well worth considering though it diverges from our purposes here. See *The Source of Life,* 87-8.
33. SBW I, 205.
34. *Either/Or,* 147. See 38-9 for the full quotation. Princeton, NJ: Princeton University Press, 1987. With Kierkegaard, it is always important to note his dialectical style, which is why it is best to emphasize that this is written from Aesthete's point of view.
35. SBW I, 205.
36. SBW I, 218.
37. SBW I, 220.
38. Ibid., 221.
39. Augustine: *Si comprehendis, no est deus.* "If you grasp/understand it, it is not God." Sermon 117.
40. Ibid., 229.
41. SBW I, 229.
42. Ibid.
43. Ibid., 231.
44. Ibid., 338.
45. *Samuel Beckett's Real Silence,* 101. The Pennsylvania State University Press,1981.
46. Ibid., 70.
47. SBW I, 338.
48. SBW II, 35.
49. *Samuel Beckett's Real Silence,* 28. The Pennsylvania State University Press, 1981.
50. SBW II, 35-6.
51. SBW II, 44.
52. *Back to Beckett,* 85. Princeton: Princeton University Press, 1973.
53. SBW II, 44.
54. *On Religion,* 82; Terrence Tice trans. Richmond, VA: John Knox Press, 1969.
55. Ibid., 79.
56. SBW II, 7.
57. SBW II, 10.
58. SBW II, 21.
59. SBW II, 19-20.
60. SBW II, 22.
61. SBW II, 32.
62. Michael Robinson explains: "The Occasionalists attempted to solve the problematic legacy of Descartes by attributing all reciprocity between mind and body to the miraculous intervention of the deity." *The Long Sonata of the Dead: A Study of Samuel Beckett,* 89. New York: Grove Press,1969.
63. SBW II, 46.
64. SBW II, 54.
65. SBW II, 55.
66. *Waiting for God,* 67. New York: Harper & Row Publishers, 1951.
67. Ibid., 71.
68. Ibid., 76.

69. Ibid., 50-1.
70. Ibid., 75.
71. SBW II, 61.
72. Quoted in *Samuel Beckett's Real Silence,* 11. The Pennsylvania State University Press, 1981.
73. *Waiting for God,* 69. New York: Harper & Row Publishers, 1951.
74. Ibid., 5.
75. SBW II, 58-9.
76. SBW II, 26.
77. SBW II, 60.
78. SBW II, 73.
79. SBW II, 3.
80. SBW II, 63.
81. SBW II, 85.
82. SBW II, 94.
83. Ibid., 96.
84. Ibid., 100.
85. Ibid., 134-5.
86. Ibid., 141.
87. Ibid., 143.
88. SBW II, 97.
89. *The Man Who Crucified Himself* by Maria Böhmer.
90. SBW II, 161.
91. Ibid., 164.
92. Ibid., 170.
93. *Samuel Beckett: The Critical Heritage,* 266-271. London: Routledge & Kegan Paul Ltd, 1979.
94. Quoted in Barge: *God, the Quest, the Hero,* 322. Chapel Hill, NC: North Carolina University Press, 1988.
95. *Church Dogmatics* III/4, 34; emphasis mine. New York; London: T&T Clark, 2004.
96. *Church Dogmatics* II/1, 240. New York; London: T&T Clark, 2004.
97. *Dynamics of Faith,* 22. New York: Harper & Row Publishers, 1957.
98. *Experiences in Theology,* xv. Minneapolis, MN: Fortress Press, 2000.
99. Ibid., xvii.

4. I Can't Go On, I'll Go On

1. https://www.nobelprize.org/prizes/literature/1969/ceremony-speech/ Accessed November 22, 2020.
2. *The Shape of Chaos,* 230. Minneapolis: The University of Minnesota Press, 1971.
3. *In the End—The Beginning,* 90. Minneapolis, MN: Fortress Press, 2004.
4. *Samuel Beckett: Poet & Critic,* 157. Princeton: Princeton University Press, 1970.
5. *Samuel Beckett: The Critical Heritage,* 244. London: Routledge & Kegan Paul Ltd, 1979.
6. *Samuel Beckett: Playwright & Poet,* 120. Ed. by Christopher Murray. New York: Pegasus Books, 2009.
7. Ibid., 120-1.
8. *The Philosophy of Samuel Beckett,* 61. London: Calder Publications, 2001.
9. *Prophetic Imagination,* 65. Minneapolis, MN: Fortress Press, 1978.

10. *Calvin's New Testament Commentaries (vol. 12),* 157. Grand Rapids, MI: Wm. B. Eerdmans Publishing Company, 1970.
11. *Prophetic Imagination,* 65. Minneapolis, MN: Fortress Press, 1978.
12. *In the End—The Beginning,* 90. Minneapolis, MN: Fortress Press, 2004.
13. *Theology of Hope,* 21. Minneapolis, MN: Fortress Press, 1993.
14. *The Courage to Be,* 164. New Haven: Yale University Press, 1952.
15. Ibid., 66.
16. Ibid., 147.
17. Ibid., 147-8.
18. Ibid., 156.
19. *The Letters of Samuel Beckett: 1929-1940,* 274. Emphasis mine. Cambridge: Cambridge University Press, 2009.
20. *Disjecta,* 68. New York: Grove Press, 1984.
21. *The Living God and the Fullness of Life,* 199. Louisville: Westminster John Knox Press, 2015.
22. SBW II, 128
23. SBW II, 359.
24. SBW IV, 435.
25. SBW IV, 446.
26. SBW IV, 471.
27. *Samuel Beckett: Playwright & Poet,* 127. Ed. by Christopher Murray. New York: Pegasus Books, 2009.
28. SBW II, 248.
29. SBW II, 296-7.
30. SBW II, 304.
31. SBW II, 332.
32. SBW II, 333.
33. *Samuel Beckett's Novel* Watt, 30n57. Philadelphia: University of Pennsylvania Press, 1984.
34. SBW III, 117.
35. SBW IV, 381.
36. Ibid.
37. *A Beckett Canon,* 308-314. Ann Arbor: The University of Michigan Press, 2001.
38. SBW IV, 390.
39. Ibid., 397.
40. Ibid., 396.
41. SBW IV, 392.
42. Ibid., 391.
43. Ibid., 384.
44. Ibid., 385.
45. Ibid., 398.
46. Ibid., 389. See Cohn: *Back to Beckett,* 144. Princeton: Princeton University Press, 1973.
47. Translated in Tonning, *Samuel Beckett's Abstract Drama,* 185-5. Bern: Peter Lang, 2007.
48. *Beckett at 60,* 3. London: Calder and Boyars, 1967.
49. *Conversations With and About Beckett,* 21. New York: Grove Press, 1996.
50. *Samuel Beckett: A Collection of Critical Essays,* 14; emphasis mine. Englewood Cliffs, NJ: Prentice-Hall, Inc., 1965.

51. *Samuel Beckett: The Critical Heritage,* 188. London: Routledge & Kegan Paul Ltd, 1979.
52. *Jesus Christ for Today's World,* 52. Minneapolis, MN: Fortress Press, 1994.
53. James Cone's powerful reflections on the cross in the American south, *The Cross and the Lynching Tree.*
54. *My Soul Looks Back,* 63. New York: Orbis Books, 1986.
55. *The Living God and the Fullness of Life,* 50-1. Louisville: Westminster John Knox Press, 2015.
56. *The Utopia of Rules,* 89. New York: Melville House, 2015.
57. Moltmann, *The Coming of God,* 336. Minneapolis, MN: Fortress Press, 1996.
58. Harold Hobson: *Beckett at 60,* 27. London: Calder and Boyars, 1967.
59. *Suffering,* 149. Philadelphia: Fortress Press, 1975.
60. *In the End—The Beginning,* 18. Minneapolis, MN: Fortress Press, 2004.
61. *Experiences of God,* 5. Minneapolis, MN: Fortress Press, 2007.
62. *Jesus Christ for Today's World,* 143. Minneapolis, MN: Fortress Press, 1994.
63. Ibid.
64. *The Crucified God,* 272. Minneapolis, MN: Fortress Press, 1993.

Conclusion

1. *Institutes* I.11.8.
2. *The Letters of Samuel Beckett: 1957-1975,* 143. Cambridge: Cambridge University Press, 2014.
3. *Samuel Beckett: Poet & Critic,* 249. Princeton: Princeton University Press, 1970.
4. *The Letters of Samuel Beckett: 1966-1989,* 622. Cambridge: Cambridge University Press, 2016
5. *The Living God and the Fullness of Life,* 150. Louisville: Westminster John Knox Press, 2015.
6. Ibid., 174.
7. *Beckett at 60,* 24. London: Calder and Boyars, 1967.
8. SBW III, 127.

BIBLIOGRAPHY

By Beckett:

Beckett, Samuel: *Collected Shorter Plays*
—*Disjecta: Miscellaneous Writings and a Dramatic Fragment*
—*Dream of Fair to Middling Women*
—*Echo's Bones*
—*Eleuthéria*
—*Happy Days*
—*How It Is*
—*Krapp's Last Tape*
—*Mercier and Camier*
—*More Pricks Than Kicks*
—*Murphy*
—*Nohow On: Company, Ill Seen Ill Said, Worstward Ho*
—*The Collected Poems of Samuel Beckett*
—*The Collected Works of Samuel Beckett,* 4 Vols.
—*The Complete Short Prose, 1929-1989*
—*The Letters of Samuel Beckett,* 4 Vols.
—*Three Novels: Molloy, Malone Dies, The Unnamable*
—*Waiting for Godot*
—*Watt*

On Beckett:

Amiran, Eyal: *Wandering and Home: Beckett's Metaphysical Narrative*
Auster, Paul: *The Art of Hunger: Essays, Prefaces, Interviews, the Red Notebook*
Badiou, Alain: *On Beckett*
Bailey, Iain: *Samuel Beckett and the Bible*
Bair, Deirdre: *Samuel Beckett: A Biography*
Baldwin, Hélèn L.: *Samuel Beckett's Real Silence*
Barge, Laura: *God, the Quest, the Hero: Thematic Structures in Beckett's Fiction*
Beja, Morris; S. E. Gontarski, Pierre Astier: *Samuel Beckett: Humanistic Perspectives*
Bloom, Harold: *Bloom's Modern Critical Views: Samuel Beckett—New Edition*
—*The Anatomy of Influence: Literature as a Way of Life*
—*The Western Canon: The Books and School of the Ages*
Boulter, Jonathan: *Beckett: A Guide for the Perplexed*
Büttner, Gottfried: *Samuel Beckett's Novel* Watt
Bryden, Mary: *Samuel Beckett and the Idea of God*
Calder, John: *As No Other Dare Fail: For Samuel Beckett on His 80th Birthday,* editor
—*Beckett at 60: A Festschrift,* editor
—*The Philosophy of Samuel Beckett*
—*The Theology of Samuel Beckett*
Carville, Conor: *Samuel Beckett and the Visual Arts*
Casanova, Pascale: *Samuel Beckett: Anatomy of a Literary Revolution*
Coe, Richard N.: *Samuel Beckett*
Cohn, Ruby: *A Beckett Canon*
—*A Casebook on* Waiting for Godot, editor
—*Back to Beckett*
—*Samuel Beckett: The Comic Gamut*
Cronin, Anthony: *The Last Modernist: Samuel Beckett*
Dukes, Gerry: *Samuel Beckett*
Esslin, Martin: *Samuel Beckett: A Collection of Critical Essays,* editor
—*The Theatre of the Absurd*

Feldman, Matthew; Karim Mamdani: *Beckett/Philosophy*
Fletcher, John: *Samuel Beckett's Art*
—*The Novels of Samuel Beckett*
Geulincx, Arnold: *Ethics: With Samuel Beckett's Notes*
Glass, Philip: *Words Without Music*
Gontarski, S. E.: *On Beckett: Essays and Criticism,* editor
—*The Intent of Undoing in Samuel Beckett's Dramatic Texts*
—*The Journal of Beckett Studies*
Graver, Lawrence; Raymond Federman: *Samuel Beckett: The Critical Heritage*
Gussow, Mel: *Conversations With and About Beckett*
Harvey, Lawrence E.: *Samuel Beckett: Poet and Critic*
Helsa, David H.: *The Shape of Chaos: An Interpretation of the Art of Samuel Beckett*
Hulle, Dirk Van; Mark Nixon: *Samuel Beckett's Library*
Jacobsen, Josephine; William R. Mueller: *The Testament of Samuel Beckett*
Joyce, James: *A Portrait of the Artist as a Young Man*
—*Dubliners*
—*Finnegans Wake*
—*Ulysses*
Juliet, Charles: *Conversations with Samuel Beckett and Bram van Velde*
Keller, John Robert: *Samuel Beckett and the Primacy of Love*
Kenner, Hugh: *A Reader's Guide to Samuel Beckett*
—*Samuel Beckett: A Critical Study*
Knowlson, James; John Pilling: *Frescoes of the Skull: The Later Prose and Drama of Samuel Beckett*
Knowlson, James: *Damned to Fame: The Life of Samuel Beckett*
Knowlson, James and Elizabeth: *Beckett Remembering Remembering Beckett: A Celebration,* editors
McDonald, Rónán: *The Cambridge Introduction to Samuel Beckett*
Morin, Emilie: *Beckett's Political Imagination*
Murray, Christopher: *Samuel Beckett: Playwright & Poet,* editor
Pilling, John: *Beckett Before Godot*
—*Samuel Beckett*
—*The Cambridge Companion to Beckett,* editor
Ricks, Christopher: *Beckett's Dying Words: The Clarendon Lectures 1990*

Robinson, Michael: *The Long Sonata of the Dead: A Study of Samuel Beckett*
Rosset, Barney: *Dear Mr. Beckett: Letters from the Publisher*
States, Bert O.: *The Shape of Paradox: An Essay on* Waiting for Godot
Tucker, David: *Samuel Beckett and Arnold Geulincx: Tracing 'A Literary Fantasia'*
Wynands, Sandra: *Iconic Spaces: The Dark Theology of Samuel Beckett's Drama*

Theology and Philosophy:

Alter, Robert: *The Hebrew Bible: A Translation with Commentary*
Augustine: *Confessions*
—*Sermons*
Barth, Karl: *Church Dogmatics,* 14 Vols.
—*Dogmatics in Outline*
—*Evangelical Theology: An Introduction*
—*The Epistle to the Romans*
—*The Humanity of God*
—*The Word of God and the Word of Man*
Barrett, William: *Irrational Man: A Study of Existential Philosophy*
Bauckham, Richard: *Moltmann: An Appreciation*
—*The Theology of Jürgen Moltmann*
Bethge, Eberhard: *Dietrich Bonhoeffer: A Biography*
Bloch, Ernst: *Atheism in Christianity*
—*The Principle of Hope,* 3 Vols.
Bonhoeffer, Dietrich: *Ethics*
—*Letters and Papers From Prison*
Busch, Eberhard: *Karl Barth: His Life from Letters and Autobiographical Texts*
Calvin, John: *Institutes of the Christian Religion,* 2 Vols.
Camus, Albert: *The Rebel*
Cioran, E. M.: *The Trouble With Being Born*
Cone, James: *A Black Theology of Liberation*
—*God of the Oppressed*
—*The Cross and the Lynching Tree*

Descartes, René: *Meditations on First Philosophy*
Enns, Peter: *Ecclesiastes (The Two Horizons Old Testament Commentary)*
—*The Sin of Certainty: Why God Desires Our Trust More Than Our "Correct" Beliefs*
Fiddes, Paul S.: *The Creative Suffering of God*
Gavrilyuk, Paul L.: *The Suffering of the Impassible God: The Dialectics of Patristic Thought*
Gutiérrez, Gustavo: *A Theology of Liberation*
Heschel, Abraham: *The Prophets*
Höffe, Otfried: *Immanuel Kant*
Hilary of Poitiers: *On the Trinity*
John of the Cross, St.: *Dark Night of the Soul*
Jüngel, Eberhard: *Death: The Riddle and the Mystery*
—*God as the Mystery of the World*
—*God's Being Is in Becoming*
Julian of Norwich: *Revelations of Divine Love*
Kant, Immanuel: *Critique of Pure Reason*
Kempis, Thomas á: *The Imitation of Christ*
Kierkegaard: *Either/Or*
—*Fear and Trembling*
—*Practice of Christianity*
Kitamori, Kazoh: *Theology of the Pain of God*
Lossky, Vladimir: *The Mystical Theology of the Eastern Church*
Marsh, Charles: *Strange Glory: The Life of Dietrich Bonhoeffer*
McCormack, Bruce L.: *Karl Barth's Critically Realistic Dialectical Theology: Its Genesis and Development 1909-1936*
McGinn, Bernard: *The Essential Writings of Christian Mysticism,* editor
Merton, Thomas: *A Thomas Merton Reader*
—*The Seven Storey Mountain: An Autobiography of Faith*
Moltmann, Jürgen: *A Broad Place: An Autobiography*
—*Experiences in Theology*
—*God in Creation*
—*In the End—The Beginning: The Life of Hope*
—*Jesus Christ for Today's World*
—*The Coming of God: Christian Eschatology*
—*The Crucified God: The Cross of Christ as the Foundation and Criticism of Christian Theology*

—*The Living God and the Fullness of Life*
—*Theology of Hope*
—*The Spirit of Life: A Universal Affirmation*
—*The Spirit of Hope*
—*The Trinity and the Kingdom*
—*The Way of Jesus Christ*
Morrison, Stephen D.: *James Cone in Plain English*
—*Jürgen Moltmann in Plain English*
—*Karl Barth in Plain English*
—*Schleiermacher in Plain English*
Nicholas of Cusa: *On Learned Ignorance*
—*On God As Not-Other: A Translation and Appraisal of De Li Non Aliud*
—*The Vision of God*
Pascal, Blaise: *Pensées*
Pelikan, Jaroslav: *The Christian Tradition: A History of the Development of Doctrine,* 5 Vols.
Prestige, G. L.: *God in Patristic Thought*
Rollins, Peter: *How (Not) to Speak of God*
Schleiermacher, Friedrich D. E.: *Christian Faith*
—*On Religion: Addresses in Response to Its Cultured Critics*
—*Servant of the Word: Selected Sermons of Friedrich Schleiermacher*
Schopenhauer, Arthur: *Essays and Aphorisms*
—*The Word as Will and Representation,* 2 Vols.
Soelle, Dorothee: *Suffering*
—*Theology for Skeptics*
—*Thinking About God*
Staniloae, Dumitru: *Orthodox Dogmatic Theology,* 6 Vols.
Teresa of Avila, St.: *Interior Castle*
The Cloud of Unknowing
Thielicke, Helmut: *The Hidden Question of God*
Tillich, Paul: *Dynamics of Faith*
—*My Search for Absolutes*
—*Systematic Theology,* 3 Vols.
—*The Courage To Be*
Torrance, T. F.: *Karl Barth: An Introduction to His Early Theology 1910-1931*

—*The Trinitarian Faith: The Evangelical Theology of the Ancient Catholic Church*
Ware, Timothy: *The Orthodox Church*
Weil, Simone: *Waiting for God*
Žižek, Slavoj; John Milbank: *The Monstrosity of Christ: Paradox or Dialectic?*
Žižek, Slavoj: *The Fragile Absolute: Or, Why is the Christian Legacy Worth Fighting For?*

ALSO BY STEPHEN D. MORRISON

Plain English Series:

Karl Barth in Plain English (2017)

T. F. Torrance in Plain English (2017)

Jürgen Moltmann in Plain English (2018)

Schleiermacher in Plain English (2019)

James Cone in Plain English (2020)

Selected bibliography:

Welcome Home: The Good News of Jesus (2016)

10 Reasons Why the Rapture Must be Left Behind (2015)

We Belong: Trinitarian Good News (2015)

For a full list of titles, visit:

www.SDMorrison.org

www.ingramcontent.com/pod-product-compliance
Lightning Source LLC
LaVergne TN
LVHW012340100826
845148LV00018B/3081

* 9 7 8 1 6 3 1 7 4 1 7 9 1 *